Cambridge Elements ≡

Elements in Philosophy and Logic
edited by
Bradley Armour-Garb
SUNY Albany
Frederick Kroon
The University of Auckland

GÖDEL'S INCOMPLETENESS THEOREMS

Juliette Kennedy
University of Helsinki

CAMBRIDGE
UNIVERSITY PRESS

CAMBRIDGE
UNIVERSITY PRESS

University Printing House, Cambridge CB2 8BS, United Kingdom

One Liberty Plaza, 20th Floor, New York, NY 10006, USA

477 Williamstown Road, Port Melbourne, VIC 3207, Australia

314–321, 3rd Floor, Plot 3, Splendor Forum, Jasola District Centre, New Delhi – 110025, India

103 Penang Road, #05–06/07, Visioncrest Commercial, Singapore 238467

Cambridge University Press is part of the University of Cambridge.

It furthers the University's mission by disseminating knowledge in the pursuit of education, learning, and research at the highest international levels of excellence.

www.cambridge.org
Information on this title: www.cambridge.org/9781108986991
DOI: 10.1017/9781108981972

First published 2022

A catalogue record for this publication is available from the British Library.

ISBN 978-1-108-98699-1 Paperback
ISSN 2516-418X (online)
ISSN 2516-4171 (print)

Gödel's Incompleteness Theorems

Elements in Philosophy and Logic

DOI: 10.1017/9781108981972
First published online: March 2022

Juliette Kennedy
University of Helsinki
Author for correspondence: Juliette Kennedy, juliette.kennedy@helsinki.fi

Abstract: This Element takes a deep dive into Gödel's 1931 paper giving the first presentation of the Incompleteness Theorems, opening up completely passages in it that might possibly puzzle the student, such as the mysterious footnote 48a. It considers the main ingredients of Gödel's proof – arithmetization, strong representability, and the Fixed Point Theorem – in a layered fashion, returning to their various aspects – semantic, syntactic, computational, philosophical, and mathematical – as the topic arises. It samples some of the most important proofs of the Incompleteness Theorems, for example, due to Kuratowski, Smullyan, and Robinson, as well as newer proofs, also of other independent statements, due to Friedman, Weiermann, and Paris-Harrington. It examines the question whether the incompleteness of, for example, Peano Arithmetic immediately gives the undecidability of the *Entscheidungsproblem*, as Kripke has recently argued. It considers set-theoretical incompleteness, and finally considers some of the philosophical consequences considered in the literature.

Keywords: Gödel, First Incompleteness Theorem, Second Incompleteness Theorem, Fixed Point Theorem, Diagonalization

ISBNs: 9781108986991 (PB), 9781108981972 (OC)
ISSNs: 2516-418X (online), 2516-4171 (print)

Contents

Introduction

The life of the mathematician is governed by the following two simple principles: for any mathematical assertion A, if it has a proof it is true, and conversely, if A is true – that is, if A is to be granted the status of a *theorem* – A must have a proof.

Into this neat correspondence between mathematical truth and mathematical proof, indeed into this soundest and most venerable of all the human sciences, namely mathematics, Gödel introduced a small, filament-like crack – albeit with a number of essential caveats. And whether mathematicians will ever have to face the consequences of Gödel's theorems, or whether a *cordon sanitaire* exists around mathematics, immunizing its core areas from the effects of incompleteness, as some have conjectured,[1] the fact is that mathematics had changed forever after 1931 – for those who cared to ponder the matter.

The Incompleteness Theorems: what are they about? What do they say about the mathematician's everyday concept of truth – not to mention everyone else's? Do the Incompleteness Theorems have even broader implications, for example for the computational nature of the mind, or for quantum physics, or, as some have suggested, for the organization of society and the logical consistency of self-government? Concerning the proof, which is based on the Liar Paradox, is it a "parlor trick," as Gödel suggested to Kreisel on a walk one day?[2] Or is it a masterpiece of logical methodology?

The logician has questions of their own: are the Incompleteness Theorems fundamentally about self-reference, about the existence of fixed points for formulae in, say, the language of arithmetic? Do they rely essentially on diagonalization and paradoxes? Or are there diagonal/self-reference–free proofs of them? Can semantic notions such as truth and definability be eliminated from the statement of the theorems and their proofs and, if so, are the syntactic versions purely syntactic? How tied to the language of arithmetic, or indeed to any particular language, are they? To which formal systems do they apply?

In this Element we weigh in on the logician's sharper questions, setting aside the broader questions raised by political scientists, theologians, and others.[3] In spite of Gödel's early worries about their generality, the Incompleteness Theorems have turned out to be incredibly plastic, appearing in as many different (dis)guises and with as many different proofs as a Greek god in pursuit of *amour*: syntactic, semantic, abstract or logic-free, liar-free, language-free, "honest," that is, such that coding and representability are presented in

---

[1]　See Macintyre's [92].
[2]　See Kreisel's Royal Society obituary of Gödel [80].
[3]　An exception is the Lucas–Penrose debate, which we (briefly) take up in Section 8.

complete detail; "mathematical," treelike, arithmetic, nonarithmetic, proof by recursively inseparable sets, proof by undecidability of the halting problem, and so forth. And although both theorems are slightly *unstable*, in the sense that with a little logical trickery in the form of so-called deviance, for example, deviant provability predicates, or deviant notation systems, they can be made to fail,[4] they are at the same time remarkably robust.

Of particular interest to us is the classification of the various proofs of the Incompleteness Theorems into the categories of syntactic and semantic – categories, as we have argued elsewhere, that can be somewhat changeable.[5] Accordingly we here explore the phenomenology of the syntax/semantics distinction, as seen through the prism of the Incompleteness Theorems. About the semantic concept of truth in particular, it is striking that in spite of his embrace of truth as a primitive notion in the 1940s, Gödel goes to great lengths to banish the concept of truth from the proof of the Incompleteness Theorems – in deference, as he would later admit, to the anti-metaphysical tenor of the times. We will also emphasize the role the theorems played in the transition in logic, and especially in set theory, from a type-theoretic framework to a first-order one. Gödel's *1931*[6] very evidently tracks this change.

If one looks back *comprehensively* on the logic of the 1920s, one can detect slight indications coming from here and there that something on the order of Gödel's *1931* was coming, especially from E. Post, and, for the Second Incompleteness Theorem, from Kuratowski.[7] It must be said, however, that many logicians, including Hilbert, hoped and indeed expected the opposite of the results of *1931*. All of this would be swept aside; on the side of premonition, the technical machinery Gödel invented for the proof went far beyond what had been done to date; and on the side of those expecting to achieve the goals of the Hilbert Program, the proof left no doubt that the desiderata of that Program, as stated, could not be carried out—shaking that program to its foundations, as Kleene would write, without quite demolishing it.[8]

It is hard to imagine the undeveloped state of logic prior to 1931 – or nearly so, considering Tarski's 1926–8 Warsaw seminar on the elimination of quantifiers, if not the Polish School in logic altogether; or considering Gödel's 1929 doctoral thesis. Computability theory, which is intimately bound up with the two Incompleteness Theorems, was in its infancy—in fact Gödel's *1931* was a

---

[4] See Section 4.1.
[5] See [72].
[6] Throughout this Element we follow the numeration of Gödel's papers as given in the *Collected Works*, vols. I–V. So "*1931*" refers to Gödel's 1931 paper, while "1931" refers to the year 1931.
[7] See Section 5.1.
[8] [42], p. 127.

central stimulus for the development of that field. The notion of a formal semantics or even the logical notion of a model did not exist at the time, although
semantic notions were relied on *sotto voce*, more or less, to wit: the structure
of the natural numbers as it is put to use in Gödel's thesis, and, more overtly,
albeit "piecewise" in Theorems V, IX, and X of Gödel's *1931*. The notion of
truth was famously and vociferously campaigned against by, for example, the
Vienna Circle, even so that the everyday mathematician could still entertain
the idea that in mathematics, truth simply meant the same thing as proof—and
indeed for today's intuitionist this remains so. Logicians conflated first- and
second- (or higher) order logic, which Gödel's 1929 Completeness Theorem
definitively separates. Finally, the concept of "finite computation" was not well
understood. Gödel and Herbrand in particular expressed doubts that an adequate definition of the concept could be given, doubts which were only put to
rest in Gödel's mind in 1936 with the advent of the Turing Machine.

On the level of syntax and semantics, one would be hard-pressed to find
the distinction laid out in, for example, Russell and Whitehead's *Principia*,
which is essentially an interpreted system, whereas Gödel's *1931* draws a
sharp distinction between the two.[9] Here is Gödel patiently (or perhaps impa-
tiently) explaining the distinction between name and referent in a 1931 letter
to Zermelo, himself a figure of colossal importance for logic and set theory, in
response to Zermelo's questioning the proof of the Incompleteness Theorems:

> Namely, one can not set
>
> $$n \in K^* = \overline{[R(n); n]},$$
>
> because the symbol complex $[R(n); n]$ has no meaning. A negation stroke,
> after all, only has meaning with reference to a symbol complex that expresses
> an assertion (with reference to the number 5, say, a negation stroke is mean-
> ingless). But the symbol complex "$[R(n); n]$" does *not* express an *assertion*.
> "$[R(n); n]$" means about the same as the following [English] words: "that
> formula of *Principia Mathematica* which results from the n-th class sign by
> substitution of the number n for the variable." "[R(n);n]" is not itself that for-
> mula ... those words, however, obviously express no assertion, but are rather
> the unique characterization of a formula (that is, of a spatial figure), just as,
> say, the words "the first formula of that book" express no assertion, even
> if perhaps the formula that is characterized by those words does express an

---

[9] Grattan-Guinness in [52], p. 296 describes the situation thus.

   Despite the attention given to the distinction between theory and metatheory in the
   1920s with Hilbert's revival of his proof theory, logicians still tended to conflate symbol and referent; indeed, Professor J. Barkley Rosser once told me in reminiscence
   that it was only with Gödel's theorem that logicians realised how careful they needed
   to be in this matter.

assertion. For each particular number n, "$[R(n); n]$" thus is a name (a unique description) for a particular formula (i.e., a spatial figure), and a negation stroke over it therefore has just as little meaning as [it would], say, over the formula "$5 + n$," which, for every number n, is a name for a particular natural number. The whole difficulty obviously is due to the fact that in metamathematics there are, besides the symbols for numbers, functions, etc., also symbols for formulas, and that one must clearly distinguish a symbol that denotes a formula from that formula itself.[10]

Does mathematics remember what happened to it in 1931? Almost 100 years after their publication, the Incompleteness Theorems appear to have had a minor impact on the life of the working mathematician. What the theorems have to say about the undecidability of certain Diophantine equations, for example, has not really come to the surface outside of logic, if it ever will.

Mathematics goes on in spite of those theorems – a testament, perhaps, to its great structural stability.

---

[10] [47], pp. 425–427.

THE FIRST INCOMPLETENESS THEOREM

1 The First Version of the Proof

Gödel's proof of the First Incompleteness Theorem asks the viewer to shift their perspective back and forth, from semantics to syntax and back again to semantics, and back again to syntax. It is a hall of mirrors such as had never before been seen in mathematics – though diagonal arguments, of which Gödel's is a supreme example, had been around at least since the time of Cantor's proof of the uncountability of the real numbers (if not earlier).

Gödel's original, informal, and unpublished (in 1931) proof of the First Incompleteness Theorem was semantic in flavor, based as it was on the undefinability of truth versus the definability of the concept of provability with respect to the arithmetic system S in which he worked, together with the soundness of the system S. The observation is simply that the set of all S-provable sentences is a subset of the set of all sentences in the language of S true in the natural numbers – in fact the former is a definable subset of the latter. But the set of all sentences in the language of S true in the natural numbers is not definable, on pain of paradox. Thus the set of all S-provable sentences is a *proper* subset of the set of all sentences in the language of S true in the natural numbers.[11] From Gödel's 1964 letter to van Heijenoort:

> Perhaps you were puzzled by the fact that I once said an attempted relative consistency proof for analysis led to the proof of the existence of undecidable propositions and another time that the heuristic principle and the first version of the proof were those given in Sect. 7 of my 1934 Princeton lectures. But it was precisely the relative consistency proof which made it necessary to formalize either "truth" or "provability" and thereby forced a comparison of the two in this respect. By an enumeration of symbols, sentences and proofs within the given system, I quickly discovered that the concept of arithmetic truth cannot be defined in arithmetic. If it were possible to define truth in the system itself, we would have something like the liar paradox, showing the system to be inconsistent ...Note that this argument can be formalized to show the existence of undecidable propositions without giving any individual instances. (If there were no undecidable propositions, all (and only) true propositions would be provable within the system. But then we would have a contradiction.)
>
> In contrast to truth, provability in a given formal system is an explicit combinatorial property of certain sentences of the system, which is formally specifiable by suitable elementary means.[12]

Gödel's conclusion that truth cannot be defined internally in S depends on *arithmetization*, namely an injective mapping from finite strings of symbols

---

[11] See Theorem 1.0.1 for the exact proof of this remark.

[12] See [47], p. 313.

into the natural numbers $\mathbb{N}$,[13] together with the *Fixed Point Theorem*. We explain these two concepts in Sections 2.1.2 and 2.1.5 respectively. Assuming these two concepts are in place, and letting $\ulcorner \phi \urcorner$ stand for the so-called "Gödel-number" of ϕ (see below), the undefinability of truth follows:

Theorem 1.0.1 *Let $\mathcal{T}$ be the set $\{\ulcorner \phi \urcorner \mid \mathbb{N} \models \phi\}$.[14] Then there is no formula $\theta(x)$ in the language of arithmetic such that for all ϕ:*

$$\mathbb{N} \models \theta(\ulcorner \phi \urcorner) \text{ if and only if } \mathbb{N} \models \phi.$$

Proof. Assume to the contrary that there is such a $\theta(x)$. Let ϕ be a fixed point of $\neg\theta(x)$.[15] That is,

$$\mathbb{N} \models \neg\theta(\ulcorner \phi \urcorner) \text{ if and only if } \mathbb{N} \models \phi.$$

If $\mathbb{N} \models \phi$ then $\mathbb{N} \models \theta(\ulcorner \phi \urcorner)$, a contradiction, by the definition of θ. If $\mathbb{N} \models \neg\phi$ then $\mathbb{N} \models \theta(\ulcorner \phi \urcorner)$, by the definition of ϕ. This is also a contradiction, as $\mathbb{N} \models \neg\phi$ implies $\mathbb{N} \models \neg\theta(\ulcorner \phi \urcorner)$, by the choice of θ. □

With the above theorem in place, Gödel could now derive the initial version of the First Incompleteness Theorem. Thus if $\mathcal{P}$ denotes the set of all Gödel-numbers of statements provable in S (under some suitable coding of those sentences fixed in advance), and $\mathcal{T}$ is again the set $\{\ulcorner \phi \urcorner \mid \mathbb{N} \models \phi\}$, where $\ulcorner \phi \urcorner$ denotes, as above, the Gödel-number of ϕ, then:

Theorem 1.0.2 $\mathcal{P}$ *is a proper subset of* $\mathcal{T}$.

Proof. By soundness, if $\ulcorner \phi \urcorner \in \mathcal{P}$, i.e., ϕ is provable, then ϕ is true. Thus $\ulcorner \phi \urcorner$ is an element of $\mathcal{T}$, i.e., $\mathcal{P}$ is a subset of $\mathcal{T}$. $\mathcal{P}$ is definable in S by a formula in the language of S, recalling Gödel's remark above that "In contrast to truth, provability in a given formal system is an explicit combinatorial property of certain sentences of the system, which is formally specifiable by suitable elementary means." If $\mathcal{P}$ were identical to $\mathcal{T}$, then $\mathcal{T}$ would be definable in S by that same formula. But $\mathcal{T}$ is not definable by *any* arithmetic formula, by the above Theorem 1.0.1. Thus $\mathcal{P} \subsetneq \mathcal{T}$. □

The theorem that truth is undefinable in the above sense is usually attributed to Tarski, who published the proof in 1933 and the German translation in 1936 [124]. Gödel clearly had Tarski's theorem in some form already in 1930. As for the question of priority related to the theorem on the undefinability of truth,

---

[13] In this Element the notation "$\mathbb{N}$" is used to denote both the set of natural numbers and the standard model of arithmetic. It will be clear from the context which is meant.

[14] The notation "$\mathbb{N} \models \phi$" means that ϕ is true in the standard model $\mathbb{N}$.

[15] For a proof of the Fixed Point Theorem, which Gödel clearly knew in 1930, see Section 2.1.5.

Gödel refers to Tarski in a footnote added at this point in the 1965 reprinting of his 1934 Princeton Lectures, albeit somewhat acidly.[16]

In these 1934 Princeton Lectures Gödel ponders self-reference, remarking that Russell and Whitehead's prohibition of *all* self-referential statements is "too drastic."[17] He cites the Fixed Point Theorem as a counterweight, as it provides a way, given "any metamathematical property *f* which can be expressed in the system, to construct a proposition that says of itself that it has this property."[18]

Gödel inserts the "first version of the proof," as he calls it, into section 7 of his 1934 Princeton Lectures, as mentioned in the above quote. Why didn't Gödel publish this first version, or even mention it, in his 1931 paper?[19] He later ascribed this to the "philosophical prejudices of the time":

> I have explained the heuristic principle for the construction of propositions undecidable in a given formal system in the lectures I gave in Princeton in 1934 …The occasion for comparing truth and demonstrability was an attempt to give a relative model-theoretic consistency proof of analysis in arithmetic. This leads almost by necessity to such a comparison.
>
> However in consequence of the philosophical prejudices of our times 1. nobody was looking for a relative consistency proof because i[t] was considered axiomatic that a consistency proof must be finitary in order to make sense. 2. a concept of objective mathematical truth as opposed to demonstrability was viewed with greatest suspicion and widely rejected as meaningless.[20]

Gödel often spoke in this vein, that is, about the philosophical or positivistic prejudices of the time, and indeed his published proof demonstrates the great care he took in order to accommodate such prejudices. Unlike his initial, informal proof, the published proof avoids to the degree possible semantic notions such as the notion of a model, of soundness, or of satisfaction in a

---

[16] "For a closer examination of this fact see A. Tarski's papers 1933a..." [42], p. 363. For more on the question of priority with regard to the Undefinability of Truth Theorem see Feferman's [22]. See also Woleński's [138]. Gödel also may have gone some way beyond Tarski's theorem in 1931 in the matter of model-theoretic semantics, based on the evidence of the mysterious footnote 48a of *1931*. On this point see Gödel's correspondence with Zermelo in the *Collected works* [47]. We discuss footnote 48a in Section 2.4.1.

[17] [42], p. 362.

[18] [43], p. 362.

[19] The heuristic or, in Gödel's words, "nonbinding" proof sketch of the First Incompleteness Theorem that Gödel gives at the beginning of *1931* resembles more the proof from a noncomputable set given in Section 2.5.1 than the original proof, though it does employ the concept of soundness. See Gödel's correspondence with Zermelo in [47] for Gödel's use of the term "nonbinding."

[20] Gödel's unsent letter to Balas, undated, [46], p. 10.

structure.[21] The caveat "to the degree possible" is meaningful; Gödel relies on a somewhat semantic condition of ω-consistency in his proof, an assumption that was later eliminated by Rosser [113], and the published syntactic proof has other semantic aspects, which we take note of as the particular issue arises.

Feferman explains Gödel's avoidance of the concept of truth in his *1931* thus, citing the above excerpt from Gödel's unsent letter to Balas:

> Here, in a crossed-out passage in an unsent reply to an unknown graduate student, I think we have reached the heart of the matter. Despite his deep convictions as to the objectivity of the concept of mathematical truth, Gödel feared that work assuming such a concept would be rejected by the foundational establishment, dominated as it was by Hilbert's ideas. Thus he sought to extract results from it which would make perfectly good sense even to those who eschewed all nonfinitary methods in mathematics ... Even more, once Gödel realized the generality of his incompleteness results it was natural that he should seek to attract attention by formulating them for the strong theories that had been very much in the public eye: theories of types such as PM and theories of sets such as ZF (Zermelo-Fraenkel). But if the concept of objective mathematical truth would be rejected in the case of arithmetic, should not one expect an even greater negative reaction to the case of theories of types or sets? All the more reason, then, not to have any result depend on it, and no need then to express one's convictions about it.[22]

Feferman's analysis notwithstanding, there is always the (rather remote) possibility that Gödel excised the concept of truth from the First Incompleteness Theorem on the basis of hesitations of his own that he may have held at the time. Seen in this light, the First Incompleteness Theorem may provide evidence for an anti-truth stance, however short-lived.[23]

---

[21] Gödel does invoke soundness in the informal sketch of the proof given at the beginning of *1931*. Also, Gödel's Theorem V relies on the concept of "piecewise" truth in the standard model. We discuss this point below in Section 2.3.1.

[22] [24], pp. 160–161.

[23] Evidence for this is somewhat sparse in the record, but it is there. See, for example, Gödel's remark in his 1933 Cambridge address:

> The result of our previous discussion is that our axioms, if interpreted as meaningful statements, necessarily presuppose a kind of Platonism, which cannot satisfy any critical mind and which does not even produce the conviction that they are consistent.

[45], pp. 49-50. For a fuller discussion of this matter see Davis's "What did Gödel believe and when did he believe it?" [13]. See also Parsons, Platonism and mathematical intuition in Kurt Gödel's thought [107]. We do not attend here to the subtleties regarding the nature of Gödel's Platonism, its relation to truth, and in particular to what Gödel himself may have meant by the term in 1933.

Putting the role of truth aside for the moment, Gödel's piercing clarity regarding the syntactic and semantic aspects of the proof can be seen in the fact that Gödel is always scrupulous to separate those elements of the proof that, in his words, "have nothing to do with the formal system P"[24] from the formal concepts. In the instance just quoted, Gödel is observing that the concept of a number-theoretic function being defined recursively from other number-theoretic functions is, simply, formalism-independent. This as it might be called "schematic" or modular approach made it easy for logicians to generalize the proof to a range of formal *and informal* settings subsequently, an enterprise that continues vigorously to this day.

2 Gödel's "Intuitionistically Acceptable" Second Proof of the First Incompleteness Theorem

2.1 Ingredients of the Proof

In our presentation of Gödel's 1931 proof we largely conform to Gödel's original presentation, though we adopt, as is usually done, a first-order setting rather than working in type theory. For a treatment of the proof including any details omitted here the reader is referred to Lev Beklemishev's brilliant survey [4], and to Kleene's introduction to [40], two of the deepest commentaries on the Incompleteness Theorems in the ocean of literature on them.

The formal system for which the Incompleteness Theorems were proved is a version of the simple (unramified) theory of types with the (second-order) Peano axioms adjoined. Using rather *PA* as the base theory,[25] the ingredients of the proof are as follows.

2.1.1 ω-consistency

We let $\bar{n}$ stand for the numeral term $s(s(\cdots s(\bar{0})\cdots))$, where s is the successor function symbol of the theory *PA*, the number of applications of the function s is n, and $\bar{0}$ denotes the constant term zero. We now state the definition of ω-consistency.

Definition 2.1.1 Let T be a theory extending *PA*.[26] We say that T is ω-*consistent* if it is not the case that there is a formula $\phi(x)$ in the language of T such that the following hold simultaneously:

---

[24] [40], p. 157.
[25] See the Glossary for the signature of *PA*, and a list of the Peano axioms.
[26] Alternatively, T can also be one of the *weaker* theories Q or R. See the Glossary for the definition of Q and R.

(i) $T \vdash \exists x \phi(x)$.

(ii) For all n, $T \vdash \neg \phi(\overline{n})$.

Note that ω-consistency is weaker than (the semantic condition of) soundness; at the same time it is stronger than (the syntactic condition of) mere consistency. Of course, ω-consistency implies consistency.

2.1.2 Arithmetization/Gödel-Numbering

Arithmetization (a.k.a. Gödel-numbering) is a one-to-one mapping of finite formal strings of the language of *PA* into the natural numbers. In Gödel's 1931 coding every element of the signature is assigned a distinct odd number; strings of symbols are then encoded with the help of the prime numbers via the mapping: $\langle n_1, n_2, \ldots, n_k \rangle \mapsto 2^{n_1} \cdot 3^{n_2} \cdots p_k^{n_k}$, where p_k is the k-th prime. In this way any formula or sentence ϕ corresponds to a number, its Gödel-number $\ulcorner \phi \urcorner$; and given any natural number, the formula it encodes (if the number is the Gödel-number of a formula) can be recovered from its Gödel-number because of prime factorization. Now it is easy to see that finite sequences of formulas can be encoded; notably, finite *proofs* can now be assigned a Gödel-number.

When it comes to the *definability* of coding, there is a subtlety here involving the β-function, so-called (see below). The above coding is not in any obvious way definable (unless we have the exponential function in the vocabulary) and while the (iterated) Cantor pairing function can be used to encode a finite sequence of any given length n, for each n the formula used to encode the sequence is different.[27] However with the β-function one has a single formula in plus and times that can encode sequences of any given length. Gödel uses the β-function later in the paper to show that the undecidable sentences constructed therein are arithmetic.

2.1.3 Primitive Recursion

Gödel defines the class of primitive recursive functions, as they are now known, or, as Gödel calls them, the "recursive" functions. In contrast to Gödel-numbering, which was a complete innovation at the time, primitive recursion was known.[28] The primitive recursive functions are defined as follows:

---

[27] See Section 2.3.1 for the definition and an application of the β-function.

[28] The phrase "primitive recursive" was coined by Rózsa Péter in 1928, the year Wilhelm Ackermann proved the existence of a recursive function that is not primitive recursive. See [3]. The primitive recursive functions appear as early as in Richard Dedekind's 1888 *What are numbers and what should they be?* [17].

Definition 2.1.2 A function f from $\mathbb{N}^n$ to $\mathbb{N}$ is an *initial function* if it is either a

(i) constant function, that is, one of: $f(x_1, x_2, \ldots, x_n) = k$, $k \in \mathbb{N}$,
(ii) projection function, that is, one of: $f(x_1, x_2, \ldots, x_n) = x_i$, $1 \le i \le n$,
(iii) the successor function: $f(x) = x + 1$.

A function f is said to be *defined by primitive recursion* from functions g and h if

$$f(0, x_1, x_2, \ldots, x_m) = g(x_1, x_2, \ldots, x_m),$$
$$f(n + 1, x_1, x_2, \ldots, x_m) = h(n, f(n, x_1, x_2, \ldots, x_m), x_1, x_2, \ldots, x_m).$$

A function f from $\mathbb{N}^k$ to $\mathbb{N}$ is *primitive recursive* (p.r.) if it is an initial function or if it belongs to the class of functions obtained by closing the initial functions under the operations of composition and primitive recursion.

An n-ary relation is said to be primitive recursive if its characteristic function is.

After proving some basic theorems about primitive recursion, Gödel then shows directly, that is, without the use of the β-function (see below), that the 45 metamathematical relations and functions needed for the first incompleteness theorem are primitive recursive. This follows from the fact that they can all be seen to be constructed according to the procedures given in his Theorems I–IV, or by finite iterations of them.[29] For example, "formula," "axiom," "immediate consequence," and, crucially, *"substitution,"* are all primitive recursive. The 46th relation, *Bew(x)*, or "x is the Gödel number of a provable formula," is of Σ_1-form, that is, it has the form of a primitive recursive predicate "$B(y, x)$" or "y is the Gödel-number of a proof of the formula with Gödel-number x" preceded by an (unbounded) existential quantifier.[30]

2.1.4 Strong Representability or, in Gödel's Terminology, "Decidability"

Gödel now shows in what is Theorem V[31] of the paper that the primitive recursive functions and relations are what he will call *decidable* in *PA* or, as is said now, *strongly representable*:[32]

Theorem 2.1.3 (Theorem V) *Let R be an k-ary primitive recursive relation. Then there is a formula $\phi_R(x_1, \ldots, x_k)$ in the language of PA such that:*

---

[29] [42], p. 159.
[30] *B* and *Bew* stand for *Beweis* and *Beweisbar* respectively. For the definition of the arithmetic hierarchy, of which of Σ_1 formulas are a part, see Section G.5.
[31] In this book we follow Gödel's numeration of the theorems in the paper *1931*. E.g., Gödel's decidability theorem is Theorem V; the First Incompleteness Theorem is Theorem VI; the Second Incompleteness Theorem is Theorem XI.
[32] Other names for decidability include "binumerable" and "numeralwise expressible."

(i) $R(n_1, \ldots, n_k)$ implies $PA \vdash \phi_R(\overline{n_1}, \ldots, \overline{n_k})$.
(ii) $\neg R(n_1, \ldots, n_k)$ implies $PA \vdash \neg\phi_R(\overline{n_1}, \ldots, \overline{n_k})$.

Gödel proves Theorem V by induction on the degree of ϕ, where the degree of a primitive recursive function is defined to be the length of the shortest sequence of number-theoretic functions ϕ_i occurring in the primitive recursive definition of ϕ.

This is a decisive moment in the proof, as with Theorem V Gödel can now show, in one fell swoop, that the forty-five constructively defined, primitive recursive relations defined in the previous step are strongly representable in *PA*. As Kleene puts it in his introductory essay,[33] Gödel's strategy here is to "mass produce" the strong representability of each of the forty-five relations he needs for the main theorem, by simply proving that *any* primitive recursive relation is strongly representable in his system.

2.1.5 The Fixed Point Theorem

The Fixed Point Theorem, also called the Diagonalization Lemma, was not isolated as an independent theorem by Gödel; he only derived the particular instance of it that was needed.[34] In his Princeton Lectures *1934* Gödel proceeds as in *1931*. However, in section 7 of *1934* he refers to the theorem explicitly, crediting Carnap's [9].[35] It is easy to see that the Fixed Point Theorem does not depend on the form of the provability predicate. The only constraint on the theory *T* for which it is proved is that *T* extends Robinson's Weak Arithmetic *Q*, which is finitely axiomatizable, or the weaker theory *R*, due to Tarski,[36] which is not finitely axiomatizable. In fact even weaker theories suffice, though this may raise questions of intensional adequacy.[37]

The statement and proof of the Fixed Point Theorem are as follows:

Theorem 2.1.4 (Fixed Point Theorem) *If $\varphi(x_0)$ is a formula of PA, then there is a sentence ψ such that:*

$$PA \vdash \psi \leftrightarrow \varphi(\overline{\ulcorner \psi \urcorner}).$$

---

[33] [42], p. 131.
[34] See Section 2.3.2 for the exact place.
[35] See Gödel's footnote 23 on p. 363 of [42].
[36] The theory *R* is also due to Robinson.
[37] We discuss intensional adequacy below in Section 4.4. As it turns out, the theories *R* and *Q* are *essentially undecidable*, meaning that every consistent extension having the same constants is undecidable. See Tarski's *Undecidable theories* [125]. There is a significant literature on the minimality of *Q* and *R* with respect to the Incompleteness Theorems, in particular on the question how weak the theory can be and the First and Second Incompleteness Theorems still apply to it. [55] is a standard source.

Proof. By a "word" we mean below a string of symbols in the vocabulary of arithmetic. Let

$$sub \ = \ \{(\ulcorner w \urcorner, \ulcorner w' \urcorner, z) : \text{The word } w' \text{ is obtained by replacing}$$
$$x_0 \text{ in the word } w \text{ everywhere by the term } \bar{z}\}.$$

It is easy to see that this is a primitive recursive relation on natural numbers. By strong representability there is a formula $\sigma(x_0, x_1, x_2)$ of *PA* such that for all natural numbers a_0, a_1, a_2:

$$(a_0, a_1, a_2) \in sub \Rightarrow PA \vdash \sigma(\overline{a_0}, \overline{a_1}, \overline{a_2}).$$
$$(a_0, a_1, a_2) \notin sub \Rightarrow PA \vdash \neg\sigma(\overline{a_0}, \overline{a_1}, \overline{a_2}).$$

W.l.o.g. x_0 is not bound in σ and x_0 and x_1 are not bound in φ. Let $\theta(x_0)$ be the formula $\exists x_1(\varphi(x_1) \wedge \sigma(x_0, x_1, x_0))$. Note that for any word w:

$$PA \vdash \theta(\overline{\ulcorner w \urcorner}) \leftrightarrow \varphi(\overline{\ulcorner w' \urcorner}), \tag{2.1}$$

where w' is obtained from w by replacing x_0 everywhere by the term $\overline{\ulcorner w \urcorner}$. Let $k = \ulcorner \theta(x_0) \urcorner$ and $\psi = \theta(\bar{k})$. Now

$$PA \vdash \psi \leftrightarrow \theta(\bar{k})$$
$$\leftrightarrow \theta(\overline{\ulcorner \theta(x_0) \urcorner})$$
$$\underset{(2.1)}{\leftrightarrow} \varphi(\overline{\ulcorner w' \urcorner}), \text{ where } w' \text{ is obtained from } \theta(x_0)$$
$$\text{by replacing } x_0 \text{ by the term } \overline{\ulcorner \theta(x_0) \urcorner} (= \bar{k})$$
$$\leftrightarrow \varphi(\overline{\ulcorner \psi \urcorner}). \qquad \square$$

We end this section with the following observation, due to Abraham Robinson [111]: the Fixed Point Theorem, in its semantic version, that is, regarded as holding in $\mathbb{N}$, is actually equivalent to Tarski's theorem on the undefinability of truth! To see this, recall that Tarski's theorem on the undefinability of truth follows from the Fixed Point Theorem. On the other hand, note that Tarski's theorem in its semantic guise states that

$$\neg \exists \theta \forall \phi (\theta(\ulcorner \phi \urcorner) \leftrightarrow \phi)$$
$$\equiv \forall \theta \exists \phi (\neg(\theta(\ulcorner \phi \urcorner) \leftrightarrow \phi))$$
$$\equiv \forall \theta \exists \phi (\neg \theta(\ulcorner \phi \urcorner) \leftrightarrow \phi),$$

where the last line exhibits a fixed point for the formula $\neg \theta$.

We make further remarks on the Fixed Point Theorem in Section 2.3.2.

2.2 The Proof

Gödel is now in a position to prove the First Incompleteness Theorem:

Theorem 2.2.1 (Theorem VI) *Let T be a theory in the language of PA satisfying:*

(i) T is axiomatizable by a primitive recursive set of axioms and rules of inference adjoined to PA.

(ii) T is ω-consistent.

Then there is a sentence ϕ in the language of T such that neither ϕ nor $\neg\phi$ is provable in T.[38]

Proof. Let $B(m,n)$ denote the relation "m is the Gödel-number of a proof in T of the formula with Gödel-number n." By assumption (*i*), this is primitive recursive. Note that $B(x,y)$ is strongly representable in T by a T-formula (i.e., a formula in the language of T) B(x,y), by Gödel's Theorem V on the strong representability of the primitive recursive predicates.[39] Following Gödel's notation, we let Bew(x) denote the T-formula $\exists y$B(y,x), and let ϕ be a sentence such that $T \vdash \phi \leftrightarrow \neg$Bew$(\ulcorner\phi\urcorner)$.

Claim 1 ϕ is unprovable in T. Assume otherwise, that is, assume $T \vdash \phi$. Then there would be a T-proof of ϕ with Gödel-number, say, n, i.e. $B(n, \ulcorner\phi\urcorner)$. By the strong representability of $B(m,n)$, we would have $T \vdash$ B$(\overline{n}, \ulcorner\phi\urcorner)$ and thus $T \vdash$ Bew$(\ulcorner\phi\urcorner)$. But then by the definition of ϕ we have $T \vdash \neg\phi$, contradicting the consistency of T.

Claim 2 $\neg\phi$ is unprovable in T. By Claim 1, for all n we have $\neg B(n, \ulcorner\phi\urcorner)$. By strong representability, for all n we have $T \vdash \neg$B$(\overline{n}, \ulcorner\phi\urcorner)$. By ω-consistency, $T \nvdash \exists y$B$(y, \ulcorner\phi\urcorner)$, that is, $T \nvdash$ Bew$(\ulcorner\phi\urcorner)$, i.e. $T \nvdash \neg\phi$. $\square$

The above theorem also holds for weaker theories. For example, as we stated above, the Fixed Point Theorem as well as Theorem V hold for Tarski's theory R, so anything as strong as R, and appropriately effective, suffices. Note that ω-consistency is only needed here for showing that the Gödel sentence is independent. The weaker version of the theorem, which establishes a true but unprovable sentence, does not require this assumption. In fact, the assumption of ω-consistency was eliminated by Rosser in 1936 [113], and replaced by the weaker notion of consistency. Rosser's generalization involves applying the Fixed Point Theorem to the formula $R(x)$: "for all z: either z is not the Gödel-number of a proof of the formula with Gödel-number x or there is a proof shorter than z of the negation of (the formula with Gödel-number) x."

---

[38] ϕ is denoted $\mathcal{G}$ in Section 2.3.3.

[39] We denote formal objects with upright typeface throughout.

2.3 Gödel's Immediate Commentary

Gödel's first comment on his proof is that the theorem is constructive, being that "all existential statements occurring in the proof are based on theorem V." A curiosity of the proof of the Decidability Theorem V (2.1.3) is that it is proved by induction on the degree of ϕ, recalling that the degree of a primitive recursive function is defined to be the length of the shortest sequence of number-theoretic functions ϕ_i occurring in the primitive recursive definition of ϕ. The concept of degree is not constructive, as Kleene shows in footnote d of his introduction to *1931*.[40] This undercuts Gödel's claim[41] that his proof of the First Incompleteness Theorem is entirely constructive, based as it is on Gödel's Theorem V, that is, his Decidability Theorem. But we can disregard this "slight blemish" on the proof, as Kleene called it.[42] Theorem V, and indeed the constructivity claim, could have been shown using induction on the structure of ϕ, which is constructive. Alternatively, as Kleene remarks in the abovementioned footnote, Gödel could have simply used the length n of the sequence of number-theoretic functions ϕ_i occurring in the primitive recursive definition of ϕ he considers in the proof, that is, not necessarily the least such n.

2.3.1 Decidability Revisited

Gödel now comments further on Theorem V, isolating its key concept, strong representability, but now in the form of an independent definition, holding of any relation, not just the primitive recursive ones.

Definition 2.3.1 Let R be an n-ary relation. R is *decidable* in a theory T in the language of *PA* if there is a formula ϕ_R in the language of T such that:

(i) $R(n_1, \ldots, n_k) \Rightarrow T \vdash \phi_R(\overline{n_1}, \ldots, \overline{n_k})$.

(ii) $\neg R(n_1, \ldots, n_k) \Rightarrow T \vdash \neg \phi_R(\overline{n_1}, \ldots, \overline{n_k})$.

Recall that in Gödel's proof of the First Incompleteness Theorem strong representability, or, as he called it, decidability, was merely a *property* of primitive recursive relations, as per Gödel's Theorem V (2.1.3). By Theorem V, then, all primitive recursive relations are strongly representable in Gödel's system, and indeed in any system extending Robinson's Q.

In his 1934 lectures Gödel introduces the wider class of general recursive functions, and proves that they are also strongly representable in the theories to

---

[40] [42], p. 132. One must presumably search through all sequences of number-theoretic functions occurring in the primitive recursive definition of ϕ in order to find the shortest such.

[41] "…we can readily see that the proof just given is constructive; that is …proved in an intuitionistically unobjectionable manner." [42], p. 177.

[42] [42], p. 131.

which the First Incompleteness Theorem applies.[43] This concept of functions strongly representable in Peano Arithmetic, namely those functions that are definable by a Σ_1 formula, would provide an alternate model of human effective computability, equivalent to Turing computability as well as all the other conceptions to date.[44] We will return to the connection between the Incompleteness Theorems and computability in Section 2.5.

In the interest of analyzing the semantic as well as the finitary content of the First Incompleteness Theorem we now prove Theorem V in the case of the exponential function $m_1^{m_2} = m_3$. We use Gödel's β-function and as usual we take Peano Arithmetic as our base theory.[45] First note that, trivially, the relations $m_1 = m_2$, $m_1 + m_2 = m_3$, and $m_1 \times m_2 = m_3$ are all strongly representable in *PA*. This follows easily from the axioms governing the behavior of these functions, and the fact that equality together with the addition and multiplication functions are part of the language of *PA*.

We now define the β-function. Recall that the Chinese Remainder Theorem states that for all relatively prime $n_1, \ldots, n_k$ and all $a_i < n_i$ ($1 \leq i \leq k$) there is a number m such that $(m, n_i) = a_i$ for $1 \leq i \leq k$, where (m, n) is the remainder when m is divided by n.[46] In a sense, the number m "codes" the sequence $a_1, \ldots, a_k$, as we can compute each a_i from m, since $a_i = (m, n_i)$. The Chinese Remainder Theorem is provable in *PA*.[47]

Let us define $\beta(m, i, n) = (m, 1 + i \cdot n)$. Note that $\beta(m_1, m_2, m_3) = m_4$ is clearly representable in *PA*. It is an easy consequence of the Chinese Remainder Theorem that for any numbers $a_1, \ldots, a_k$ there are m and n such that $\beta(m, i, n) = a_i$ for all $i = 1, \ldots, k$.

We can now represent $m_1^{m_2} = m_3$ as follows, and it is just here that we are appealing to semantic content in the form of the primitive recursive scheme defining the exponentiation function in natural language, for the construction of the formal analogue of the exponentiation function. Namely, $m_1^{m_2} = m_3$ holds if and only if there are numbers a_i, $1 \leq i \leq m_2$, such that $a_1 = m_1$, $a_{i+1} = m_1 \cdot a_i$ for $1 \leq i < m_2$, and $a_{m_2} = m_3$. (We suppress the formal symbol for numerals to facilitate ease of reading.) By the above consequence of the Chinese Remainder Theorem, $m_1^{m_2} = m_3$ holds if and only if there are

---

[43] Note that a function is strongly representable if its graph is.

[44] As can be easily seen by examining the definition of strong representability, a function is strongly representable if and only if it is defined by a Σ_1 formula. This follows from the fact that $\vdash \phi_R(\overline{n_1}, \ldots, \overline{n_k})$ is Σ_1 in $n_1, \ldots, n_k$.

[45] Gödel calls the β-function by this name only in his 1934 Princeton Lectures. As was noted instead of *PA* the base theory can be taken to be Robinson Arithmetic Q or the weaker theory R.

[46] Two natural numbers are said to be relatively prime if they have no common divisors other than 1.

[47] See [66], section 5.

numbers m and n such that $\beta(m,1,n) = m_1$, $\beta(m,i+1,n) = m_1 \cdot \beta(m,i,n)$ for $1 \leq i < m_2$, and $\beta(m,i+1,n) = m_3$. We may now conclude that $m_1^{m_2} = m_3$ is representable in PA. The proof is similar for any primitive recursive function. One simply codes the appropriate sequence by means of the β-function.

Note that nowhere in the proof of Theorem V is the full structure of the natural numbers invoked. Strong representability is proved "piecewise," that is, for a given function defined on a *finite segment* of the natural numbers. The proof is thus constructively, which at the time was usually employed by Gödel as a synonym for "finitistically,"[48] acceptable. Gödel in later years was interested in defining the limit of finitary reasoning, which for him meant finding a specific proof-theoretic ordinal. A proposal considered in the substantial literature on the limits of finitary reasoning is that *primitive recursive arithmetic (PRA)* should define that limit.[49]

As to the broader point whether the standard model is invoked in the proof of the Incompleteness Theorems, so going beyond considerations involving decidability, the following observation can be made: Gödel assumes the (syntactic) consistency of his theory. Therefore by his own Completeness Theorem (which is the result of his 1929 thesis) linking the syntactic property of consistency to the semantic condition of the existence of a model, one can now infer the existence of a model of the theory. Of course the Completeness Theorem depends on an infinitary principle, Weak König's Lemma.[50]

Is "decidability in a theory" a purely syntactic condition? It is generally thought to be so, on the basis of some mutual understanding of the term "syntactic." Gödel used the term to mean "devoid of content":[51]

> The essence of this view is that there is no such thing as a mathematical fact, that the truth of propositions which we believe express mathematical facts only means that (due to the rather complicated rules which define the meaning of propositions, that is, which determine under what circumstances

---

[48] See, e.g., [122].

[49] For the definition of *PRA* see Section G.2. We return to *PRA* as the limit of finitary reasoning in Section 8.

[50] Let $2^{<\omega}$ be the set of all finite binary sequences viewed as a tree ordered by the end-extension relation. That is, an extension of a sequence s, which is an element of the tree, is any sequence that s is an initial segment of. A subset of $2^{<\omega}$ that is closed under subsequences is called a subtree of $2^{<\omega}$. A branch of a subtree is a subset that is linearly ordered by the tree-order. *Weak König's Lemma* says that every infinite subtree of $2^{<\omega}$ has an infinite branch.

[51] For a discussion of Gödel's view of the term "content" or "contentual" and related words, see van Atten, "Natural constructive proofs of A via $A \rightarrow B$, proof paradoxes, and impredicativity," https://hal.archives-ouvertes.fr/hal-03296950/.

a proposition is true) an idle running of language occurs in these propositions, in that the said rules make them true no matter what the facts are. Such
propositions can rightly be called void of content.[52]

Returning to the question of the possible semantic content of Theorem V,
Gödel says this in footnote 41: "When this proof is carried out in detail, r [the
formal object ϕ_R JK], of course, is not defined indirectly with the help of its
meaning but in terms of its purely formal structure."[53] Beklemishev observes
on this point that:

> Gödel's notion of decidability in a theory ...does not appeal to the "con-
> tentual" meaning (*inhaltliche Deutung*) of the formulae of the system P.
> However, one can still see that this notion implicitly appeals to a seman-
> tic interpretation of primitive recursive schemes, because the formula ϕ_R is
> in fact constructed from a primitive recursive scheme defining R...[54]

In other words, the definition of the formula ϕ_R, whether in the type-theoretic
framework and/or relying on the β-function, draws on the actual primitive
recursive definition of the relation R, or, more precisely, its *meaning*. In that
sense this part of the proof may be said to have and/or express an implicit
semantic content. Of course appealing to semantic content in setting up a formal system does not mean that the resulting formal language is to be regarded
as contentual. This idea can be accommodated in logical practice via the mech-
anism of an interpretation, that is, the assignment of a (formal) semantics to the
formalism in question, and in this way "the formal" is merged with semantic
content. Otherwise one requires a notion of syntax that could accommodate an
appeal to the meanings of the pre-theoretic object in question, in the formulation
of the syntax – as seems vaguely to happen, for example, in strong representability.[55] Failing such a device, the formal analogue of the primitive recursive

---

[52] Gibbs lecture, in [45], p. 319. In draft V of the paper "Is mathematics a syntax of language?"
Gödel identifies the syntactical view with the following three assertions: First, mathematical
intuition can be replaced by conventions about the use of symbols and their application. Second,
"there do not exist any mathematical objects or facts," and therefore mathematical propositions are void of content. Third, the syntactical conception defined by these two assertions is
compatible with strict empiricism. [45], p. 356.

[53] [42], p. 173.

[54] [4], p. 7. The semantic interpretation of a primitive recursive scheme is simply the p.r. function
itself.

[55] Koellner's [77] treats Carnap's wider notion of syntax, which accommodates semantic notions,
but this is done in a way very different than what is asked for here. See also Floyd and Putnam's
[28], pp. 631–632, which the following anecdote is told:

> ...one of us (Putnam) remembers a delightful philosophical conversation between
> C.G. Hempel and one of Hans Reichenbach's graduate students in Reichenbach's
> living room in 1950, at which the older attitude and the newer attitude memorably

function, the entire formalism for that matter, is a "genealogical isolate," in the terminology of race theory – stripped of origins, stripped of meaning.[56]

We take a moment to consider Gödel's general view that semantic concepts are in this sense primary, whether meaning, or content, or, simply, truth. The following remark made at the beginning of his 1934 Princeton Lectures is an early example:

> While a formal system consists only of symbols and mechanical rules relating to them, the meaning which we attach to the symbols is a leading principle in the setting up of the system.[57]

Kleene echoes and elaborates on this point in his introduction:

> The deduction of propositions of the selected portion of mathematics, when formalized in S, consists simply of mechanical manipulations of the formal objects, with no reliance on their meanings (even though the meanings are what make the system of interest to us as mirroring informal mathematics). If we should be tempted to use something from the meanings or interpretation, what we use should have been put into the system S in the form of additional axioms or rules of inference.[58]

Kleene may be referring to the idea of syntax as a repository, of some kind, of meaning: the idea that the syntax must always speak – and speak contentually – but now in the language of axioms and rules. Or Kleene may be making a more modest point, philosophically; in setting up a formal system, the principles used informally are to be coded into the syntax in the form of formal axioms and formal rules.

As for the stronger reading, Gödel echoes the point in a 1967 letter to Wang:

> How indeed could one think of *expressing* metamathematics *in* the mathematical systems themselves, if the latter are considered to consist

---

clashed. Hempel was defending Quine's skepticism with respect to the analytic-synthetic distinction, and the graduate student said plaintively: "Quine's arguments may show that the analytic-synthetic distinction makes no sense in natural language. But why doesn't it make clear sense in a formalized language?"; and Hempel replied: "Every formalized language is ultimately explained in some natural language. The disease [Hempel meant the unclarity of the analytic-synthetic distinction] is hereditary." Here, Hempel—like Wittgenstein in *Remarks on the Foundations of Mathematics*— was denying that a formal system *could* provide us with a standard of truth or clarity that is, in principle, inaccessible to a natural language.

[56] The phrase "genealogical isolate" appears, e.g., in Patterson's *Slavery and social death: a comparative study* [108].

[57] [42], p. 349.

[58] [42], p. 126.

of meaningless symbols which acquire some substitute of meaning only *through* metamathematics?[59]

Draft V of Gödel's paper "Is mathematics a syntax of language?"[60] treats this point at length. The Beklemishev point, as we may call it, is drawn upon again and again; in order to devise the system in question, never mind to ultimately to ascertain its consistency, one needs an available content to begin with, a starting point. Conventionalism, which Gödel sees as a variant of the syntactic point of view, is here argued against; in particular Gödel argues that conventions regarding symbolic manipulation express or presuppose factual knowledge about symbols, knowledge "which must be known to us *already* in an empirical attire (i.e. mixed with synthetic facts)."[61] One can adopt the view that conventions are devoid of content in an absolute sense, but:

> If one speaks of conventions and their voidness of content in an absolute sense, this can only mean that they are conventions relative to that body of knowledge which is indispensable for making any linguistic conventions at all.[62]

These are "unequivocally ascertainable [i.e., true] relations between the primitive terms of combinatorics, such as 'pair,' 'equality,' 'iteration,' and they can least of all be eliminated by basing the use of those terms on conventions."[63]

However the account of symbolic manipulation is framed – however one views the setting up of the formal system – there is, on the opposite side of the spectrum, the issue of the consistency of the entire system, which cannot be derived internally, as a consequence of Gödel's Second Incompleteness Theorem. Gödel returns to this point again and again:[64]

---

[59] [47], pp. 397–398.
[60] *1953/9*, [45].
[61] [45], p. 342. Emphasis mine.
[62] [45], pp. 342–343.
[63] [45], footnote 32, p. 346.
[64] See also Gödel's *Dialectica* paper, which turns on the ineliminability of *meaning*:

> P. Bernays has pointed out on several occasions that, since the consistency of a system cannot be proved using means of proof weaker than those of the system itself, it is necessary to go beyond the framework of what is, in Hilbert's sense, finitary mathematics if one wants to prove the consistency of classical mathematics, or even that of classical number theory. Consequently, since finitary mathematics is defined as the mathematics in which evidence rests on what is *intuitive*, certain abstract notions are required for the proof of the consistency of number theory (as was also explicitly formulated by Bernays in his 1935, pages 62 and 69). Here, by abstract (or nonintuitive) notions we must understand those that are essentially of second or higher order, that is, notions that do not involve properties or relations of concrete objects

But now it turns out that for proving the consistency of mathematics an intuition of the same power is needed as for deducing the truth of the mathematical axioms, at least in some interpretation. In particular the abstract mathematical concepts, such as "infinite set," "function," etc., cannot be proved consistent without again using abstract concepts, i.e., such as are not merely ascertainable properties or relations of finite combinations of symbols. So, while it was the primary purpose of the syntactical conception to justify the use of these problematic concepts by interpreting them syntactically, it turns out that quite on the contrary, abstract concepts are necessary in order to justify the syntactical rules (as admissible or consistent) …the fact is that, in whatever manner syntactical rules are formulated, the power and usefulness of the mathematics resulting is proportional to the power of the mathematical intuition necessary for their proof of admissibility. This phenomenon might be called "the non-eliminability of the content of mathematics by the syntactical interpretation."[65]

Gödel's extensive arguments in favor of the inelimininability of mathematical content, in the form of meaning or in terms of other semantic concepts, appear primarily in his later writings. But we see the preoccupation already here, if not already in an embryonic form in the introduction to his 1929 thesis.[66]

2.3.2 The Fixed Point Theorem

The literature can be somewhat vague on the question whether Gödel's *1931* invokes the general Fixed Point Theorem or not. If we examine Gödel's 1931 proof, when is the fixed point taken? This is not done explicitly, that is, the fixed point is not obtained by invoking the general Fixed Point Theorem; rather, the fixed point is extracted in this particular case, and this is true also of the 1934 Princeton lectures. In the interest of evaluating the importance of self-reference in the form of fixed points for the First Incompleteness Theorem we now focus on this point. The reader may want to have [42] opened to page 175 nearby. To this end let T and $B(x,y)$ be as in the above section 2.2. Thus $B(x,y)$ "means" "x is a proof of y." Let $Num(x)$ be the function that gives the Gödel-number of the number x when x is represented as a numeral. Let $Sub(x,y,z)$ be, whenever well-defined, the Gödel-number of the expression obtained from the

---

(for example, of combinations of signs), but that relate to mental constructs (for example, proofs, meaningful statements, and so on); and in the proofs we make use of insights, into these mental constructs, that spring not from the combinatorial (spatiotemporal) properties of the sign combinations representing the proofs, but only from their *meaning*.

1958, in [43], p. 241. Emphasis in the original text.

[65] [45], p. 357.

[66] See [69] for a discussion of the philosophical content of Gödel's thesis. For further discussion of Gödel's argument against the syntactic view see also [71].

expression whose Gödel-number is x when every occurrence of the expression whose Gödel-number is y is replaced by the numeral term whose Gödel-number is z. The notation $\phi(u/v)$ denotes the formula ϕ with u substituted for the free variable v. Gödel begins his proof by defining

$$Q(x,y) \equiv \neg B(x, Sub(y, \ulcorner y_1 \urcorner, Num(y))).$$

Q is primitive recursive, hence strongly representable. Therefore there is a formula $q(x_1,y_1)^{67}$ such that for all natural numbers m, n:

$$\neg B(m, Sub(n, \ulcorner y_1 \urcorner, Num(n))) \Rightarrow T \vdash q(\overline{m}/x_1, \overline{n}/y_1) \quad (\equiv q(\overline{m}, \overline{n})),$$

$$B(m, Sub(n, \ulcorner y_1 \urcorner, Num(n))) \Rightarrow T \vdash \neg q(\overline{m}, \overline{n}).$$

Gödel now defines:

$$p = \forall x_1 q(x_1, y_1),$$

$$r = q(x_1, Num(p)/y_1).$$

Here p "says" "$Sub(y_1, \ulcorner y_1 \urcorner, Num(y_1))$", which can be informally written as $y_1(\overline{y_1}/y_1)$, is not provable." Gödel now in line 13 (of page 175) gives the following string of equalities:

$$Sub(\ulcorner p \urcorner, \ulcorner y_1 \urcorner, Num(\ulcorner p \urcorner)) = Sub(\ulcorner \forall x_1 q(x_1, y_1) \urcorner, \ulcorner y_1 \urcorner, Num(\ulcorner p \urcorner))$$

$$= \ulcorner \forall x_1 q(x_1, Num(\ulcorner p \urcorner)/y_1) \urcorner = \ulcorner \forall x_1 r(x_1) \urcorner.$$

It is just here that Gödel takes a fixed point. If we let $\psi = \forall x_1 r(x_1)$, then:

$$\psi \leftrightarrow \forall x_1 r(x_1) \leftrightarrow \forall x_1 q(x_1, Num(\ulcorner p \urcorner)/y_1)$$

$$\leftrightarrow \forall x_1 q(x_1, Sub(\ulcorner p \urcorner, \ulcorner y_1 \urcorner, Num(\ulcorner p \urcorner))) \leftrightarrow \forall x_1 q(x_1, \psi).$$

That is, as is usual in the proofs of the First Incompleteness Theorem invoking the general Fixed Point Theorem, the fixed point is taken for the formula $\forall x_1 q(x_1, y_1)$. And as one can see from the proof, the construction of the fixed point does not depend on any property of the predicate $q(x_1, y_1)$, as was mentioned, and therefore the general Fixed Point Theorem is essentially immediate, holding for any predicate expressible in T.

Logicians have found the Fixed Point Theorem, and consequently the Incompleteness Theorems – *insofar as they may be based on the Fixed Point Theorem* – somewhat mysterious.[68] As Kotlarski has written, but speaking for many: "In fact, the usual proof of the diagonal lemma …is short, but tricky

---

[67] Here, and throughout, we follow Gödel in breaking the convention of using upright font for formal objects.

[68] Even Gödel-numberings can have fixed points [50].

and difficult to conceptualize. The problem was to eliminate this lemma from proofs of Gödel's result. This was achieved only in the 1990s."[69] Others have spoken of magic,[70] or of pulling rabbits out of hats[71] and so forth. This befuddlement – if one may call it that – has spawned a flood of beautiful theorems, namely alternate, diagonal-free or close to diagonal-free, and/or self-reference–free, and finally "mathematical" proofs of the First and Second Incompleteness Theorems, which completely reconceptualize those theorems.[72] Kleene is considered to have produced the first such, involving recursively inseparable sets [76]. We will consider a number of other diagonal- and/or self-reference–free proofs[73] in Section 5.

Given the effort that has gone into eliminating diagonalization from proofs of the Incompleteness Theorems, is diagonalization really pathological? In 1873 Cantor proved [8] that there are more transcendental numbers than algebraic numbers – in fact "most" real numbers are transcendental. This follows from Cantor's diagonal argument showing that there are uncountably many real numbers, together with the fact that the algebraic numbers, being defined by a finite string of symbols drawn from a countably infinite alphabet, must be countable. This is a pure existence proof, but it raised opposition nevertheless, as can be seen from the following 1883 letter of Hermite to Mittag-Leffler. Hermite had proved the transcendentality of e at the same time that Cantor proved that most reals are transcendental:

> The impression that Cantor's memoirs makes on us is distressing. Reading them seems, to all of us, to be a genuine torture ... While recognizing that he has opened up a new field of research, none of us is tempted to pursue it. For us it has been impossible to find, among the results that can be understood, a single one having current interest. The correspondence between the points of a line and a surface leaves us absolutely indifferent and we think that this result, as long as no one has deduced anything from it, stems from such arbitrary methods that the author would have done better to withhold it and wait.[74]

---

[69] [79], p. 126.

[70] Gaifman: "The brevity of the proof does not make for transparency; it has the aura of a magician's trick" [37].

[71] McGee, Vann; "The First Incompleteness Theorem," Handouts of the Course Logic II. https://bit.ly/301QLTA "I don't know anyone who thinks he has a fully satisfying understanding of why the Self-referential Lemma works. It has a rabbit-out-of-a-hat quality for everyone."

[72] See Salehi [114] for a survey and references. Salehi also discusses diagonal-free proofs of Tarski's theorem on the undefinability of truth, and even diagonal-free proofs of the Fixed Point Theorem itself.

[73] The terms "diagonal" and "self-referential" have sometimes been used as synonyms in the literature, but of course they are not. Cantor's proof of the uncountability of the real numbers is a diagonal argument, but not a self-referential one, for example.

[74] Excerpt of letter from Hermite to Mittag-Leffler quoted in [53], p. 209.

It is not only logicians who have expressed qualms concerning diagonal arguments!

Friedman has proved a theorem that goes some way toward pinpointing the possibly problematic nature of Cantor's diagonal function. Recall that a set of real numbers is said to be *Borel* if it belongs to the smallest collection of sets of reals that contains the open sets and is closed under complements and countable unions.[75] The Borel sets are canonically well-behaved in that they have all of the so-called regularity properties; a Borel set is Lebesgue measurable, it has the property of Baire, and it has the perfect set property. The Borel sets also satisfy the continuum hypothesis; if a Borel set of reals is uncountable then it has cardinality $2^{\aleph_0}$. Friedman's theorem [33] is as follows.

Theorem 2.3.2 *There is no Borel function F(s) from infinite sequences of reals to reals such that if ran(s) = ran(s'), then F(s) = F(s'), and moreover F(s) is always outside ran(s).*

Our proof of the above theorem is due to Menachem Magidor and is unpublished, so we take the opportunity to publish it here, with his kind permission. The proof requires advanced knowledge of set theoretic techniques, such as forcing.

Proof. Suppose there is an F as stated. Let P be the so-called Levy collapse of the set of reals to ω. Namely, the conditions in P are one-to-one functions from a finite subset of ω into the reals of V. So the generic is a function from ω onto the reals of V. Let s be the code of the set of the old reals, given by the Levy collapse generic. By the Shoenfield Absoluteness Lemma, the function F (given by its Borel code) has the same property (as in the Claim), also in the forcing extension. We now show that $F(s)$ is in fact in the ground model. But then it is a member of ran(s), a contradiction.

Proof that $F(s)$ is in the ground model: $F(s)$ is a real, that is, a member of 2^ω. The value of $F(s)$ is a term in the forcing language. It is enough to show that for every n either the empty condition forces "$F(s)(n) = 0$" or the empty condition forces "$F(s)(n) = 1$." Assume otherwise. So there are conditions p, q which force respectively $F(s)(n) = 0$ and $F(s)(n) = 1$. Note that since F is a Borel function it has a natural extension to any forcing extension of V and this extension is definable from a real (the Borel code of F) in V.

---

[75] More precisely, the Borel sets can be defined by transfinite induction as follows. Let B_0 be the family of open sets of reals. Let $B_{\alpha+1}$ be the family of complements and countable unions of sets in B_α. Note that then $B_{\alpha+1}$ contains also all countable intersections of sets in B_α. If ν is a limit ordinal, let $B_\nu = \bigcup_{\alpha<\nu} B_\alpha$. The family of all Borel sets of reals is $\bigcup_{\alpha<\omega_1} B_\alpha$.

Let G_p be a generic filter containing p. Let s_p be the real which codes the list of countably many reals enumerated by G_p. By using a standard automorphism argument of the forcing notion we can find in $V[G_p]$ another V-generic filter G_q, containing q. Let s_q be the real coding the enumeration given by G_q. The range of s_p and s_q is the same, namely the set of reals of V. Hence $F(s_p) = F(s_q)$. This contradicts the fact that $p \in G_p$ forces that $F(s)(n) = 0$ and $q \in G_q$ forces $F(s)(n) = 1$. $\qquad\square$

Returning to the Fixed Point Theorem, in particular having seen the theorem at work, we press the question a last time: *Are* these diagonal proofs really inherently mysterious? It has become a matter of logical dogma that they are. One has the feeling that something is hidden – that there is a "whiff of paradox," as Davis has said [14], hanging over the proof. But there is mystery, and then there there is total blackout. That is, if we consider objects constructed on the basis of the Axiom of Choice here we have no information about the constructed object beyond its mere postulated existence. For example, by the Axiom of Choice there exists a well-ordering of the reals; however, no information about the nature of this well-ordering is delivered by that axiom. This is in contrast to the Fixed Point Theorem, where one at least has a recipe in hand for the construction of the object, however magical.

2.3.3 ω-consistency, ω-inconsistency, and Nonstandard Models of Arithmetic

Gödel's theorem (as originally stated) involves primitive recursively axiomatizable theories. Gödel notes further on in the paper that the theorem also holds for any ω-consistent theory T for which all primitive recursive relations are strongly representable, together with the assumption that the set of Gödel-numbers of the axioms of T, together with the relation "immediate consequence," are primitive recursive in T.[76]

Gödel's next observation about the proof is that assuming the system T is consistent, $\neg G$ can be consistently adjoined to T.[77] This yields a consistent, ω-*in*consistent theory T'. The possibility of a *consistent* and adequate formal system yielding false theorems, as happens here, is contrary, many would argue, to the hopes of the Hilbert Program. Among the many possible philosophical morals of the First Incompleteness Theorem, Gödel chose to stress this particular point – framed as an explicit critique of formalism – in his announcement of the proof in Königsberg in 1930. This was the occasion when, during a

---

[76] See p. 181 of [42].

[77] G is the sentence ϕ of Section 2.2.

roundtable discussion taking place on the last day of that meeting, he casually announced the First Incompleteness Theorem.[78]

What do these false theorems say? To answer this we must make a brief digression into the topic of non-standard models of arithmetic. We work in first-order Peano Arithmetic (*PA*). Gödel's Completeness Theorem combined with the First Incompleteness Theorem is equivalent to the statement that *PA* has two models which are not *elementarily equivalent*.[79] What are these models like? We know of one model of *PA*, the standard model $\mathbb{N}$. But what about the other, so-called nonstandard models? What are they like, and how many of them are there?

By the Löwenheim-Skolem Theorem we know that *PA* has models in all infinite cardinalities. If we restrict our attention to the countable models, it turns out that there are $2^{\aleph_0}$ nonisomorphic countable models of *PA*, that is, as many as possible.[80] Question: Is this plethora of models due to incompleteness, or is there another way to understand (describe) these models? In 1934 Skolem constructed the first nonstandard model of *True Arithmetic*[81] using the technique of arithmetic ultrapowers; and in 1936 Malcev [94] gave, as an easy application of the compactness theorem, the existence of a model that includes the natural numbers as an initial segment, but which also includes so-called nonstandard or infinite numbers c satisfying: $\{c > \bar{0}, c > \bar{1}, c > \bar{2}, \ldots\}$, for all natural numbers n.[82] As it turns out, the order types of all nonstandard models of *PA* look like this: an isomorphic copy of the natural numbers in their natural linear ordering, followed by the so-called nonstandard part, with a densely ordered set of copies of $\mathbb{Z}$.

Let us now consider the consistency statement for *PA*, or a particular form of it, as there are many ways to express consistency. In the notation of Section 2.2 this can be written $\forall x \neg B(x, \overline{\ulcorner 0 = 1 \urcorner})$, denoted Ψ: "for all x, x does not code a proof of the statement $0 = 1$." By Gödel's Second Incompleteness Theorem,[83]

---

[78] See *1931a* in [42], which is the postscript added to the proceedings of the meeting, solicited from Gödel by the editors of those proceedings. For a fuller account of Gödel's announcement see Dawson's introductory note to *1931a*, [42], p. 196. In Section 8 we will consider various objections to the idea that the Incompleteness Theorems undermined the goals of the Hilbert Program, especially regarding the Second Incompleteness Theorem.

[79] Two models are elementarily equivalent if they satisfy the same sentences in their shared language.

[80] See, e.g. [66], for details.

[81] True arithmetic is the theory consisting of the set of all sentences in the language of arithmetic that are true in the standard model $\mathbb{N}$.

[82] Let $\mathcal{L}$ be the language of *PA*, and let T in the augmented language $\mathcal{L} \cup c$ be obtained by adding to *PA* the axioms $\{c > \bar{0}, c > \bar{1}, c > \bar{2}, \ldots\}$. T is finitely consistent, hence, by compactness, consistent. Therefore T has a model.

[83] See the Section "The Second Incompleteness Theorem".

this is unprovable in *PA*, and therefore ¬Ψ can be consistently adjoined to *PA*, yielding a new theory *T*. By the Completeness Theorem, *T* has a model *M*. Note that ¬Ψ is an existential statement – it asserts the existence of an element *c* of *M* which codes a proof of $0 = 1$. The point is that *c* must be a nonstandard element of *M*, as we assume the consistency of *PA*. In that sense, *M* can be thought of as containing proofs which are infinite in length.

In fact by now a great deal is known about nonstandard models of Peano Arithmetic. Here is a very striking result, again restricting our attention to the countable models of *PA*. For any such model $\mathfrak{M}$, we can identify the domain of $\mathfrak{M}$ with the natural numbers; accordingly we can regard the plus and times of the model, denoted $+_{\mathfrak{M}}$ and $\cdot_{\mathfrak{M}}$, as ternary relations on the natural numbers. A theorem of Tennenbaum says that for any countable model $\mathfrak{M}$ of arithmetic, the operations $+_{\mathfrak{M}}$ and $\cdot_{\mathfrak{M}}$ cannot be *recursive*, that is, there is no procedure that, if one asks of a particular triple of natural numbers $\langle m, n, r \rangle$, whether $m +_{\mathfrak{M}} n = r$, returns a yes-or-no answer.[84] Of course we know how to add *m* and *n* if we regard *m* and *n* as names of the natural numbers that live the standard model $\mathbb{N}$. But *m* and *n* are not necessarily names of natural numbers; they are names for elements of the model $\mathfrak{M}$.

Thus if we accept only recursive models of Peano, and consider only the countable ones, Tennenbaum's Theorem shows that then Peano is categorical, in that it has only one model. But then because a categorical theory is necessarily complete, incompleteness disappears. This should raise interest in nonrecursive objects, and put a damper on the kind of talk that only recursive objects are relevant.[85]

2.4 Gödel Remarks Further on the Scope of the First Incompleteness Theorem

After making this point about the existence of nonstandard models, Gödel remarks on a special case of Theorem VI, namely when the theory in question is finite, and thus recursive. He also observes that the First Incompleteness Theorem applies to a variety of systems, including Zermelo-Fraenkel set theory

---

[84] See [66] for a proof of Tennenbaum's Theorem. As we noted, Gödel uses the term "recursive" for what is now known as "primitive recursive" in his 1931 paper. In his 1934 lectures, he introduces the term "general recursive," which is now known as "partial recursive," or, equivalently, "computable." A partial recursive (or, equivalently, computable) function that happens to be total is referred to by some as "recursive" and we adopt this terminology here. Mostowski [102] came close to proving Tennenbaum's Theorem in proving that arithmetic in a vocabulary that contains not only plus and times but also certain six primitive recursive functions has no nonstandard recursive models.

[85] See [56] for an alternative view.

and Peano Arithmetic – a mark of Gödel's continuing throughout the paper, to grapple with the scope of Theorem VI.

2.4.1 The Mysterious Footnote 48a

It was just here at the end of section 2 of the paper that Gödel is moved to explain, in a footnote, "the true reason for the incompleteness in all formal systems of mathematics." Footnote 48a of *1931* reads as follows:

> As will be shown in part II of this paper, the true reason for the incompleteness inherent in all formal systems of mathematics, is that the formation of ever higher types can be continued into the transfinite (see Hilbert [63], p. 184), while in any formal system at most denumerably many of them are available. For it can be shown that the undecidable propositions constructed here become decidable whenever appropriate higher types are added (for example, type ω to the system P). An analogous situation prevails for the axiom system of set theory.

Part II of the paper, which was to include a detailed proof of the Second Incompleteness Theorem,[86] would never materialize – but this is not our concern here. What is striking about the remark is the degree of knowledge of certain logical machinery that was completely unknown at the time. In Section 1, we noted Gödel's anticipation of Tarski's Undefinability of Truth Theorem, which is needed for the first informal proof of the First Incompleteness Theorem. Footnote 48a suggests model-theoretic knowledge going beyond this. Or what model-theoretic machinery is needed to verify the above claim for decidability of undecidable propositions in higher types?

Before turning to these questions, it may be worth pointing out that Gödel demonstrated something of a penchant throughout his career for mentioning important metamathematical results in footnotes and casual asides in lectures, without proving them. His 1946 Princeton Bicentennial Lecture [44], in which Gödel asks for absolute notions of provability and definability, is a case in point. Among the assertions there is the claim that ordinal definability is itself definable, a fact that is nowadays shown using the Levy Reflection Principle, which was proved by Levy in 1960 [88].[87] Gödel asserts, and not conjectures, here the independence of the axiom of constructibility, $V = L$.[88] Another conjecture is that HOD, the class of hereditarily ordinal definable sets, will be a model of set theory satisfying choice, giving a simpler consistency proof of

---

[86] See the section titled "The Second Incompleteness Theorem" below.

[87] The principle says that for every n there are arbitrarily large ordinals α such that $V_\alpha \prec_n V$.

[88] In this connection see Gödel's letter to Wolfgang Rautenberg of June 30, 1967, in [47], p. 183.

the Axiom of Choice (*AC*). This was proved much later, in [105].[89] Finally, Gödel predicts that the proof of *AC* in HOD will not extend to a proof of the Continuum Hypothesis (*CH*), and in fact the failure of the *CH* was shown to be consistent with $V = $ HOD in 1968. One could also point to his 1933 abstract on speed-up theorems, so-called, which were proved in complete detail by Buss only in the 1990s.[90]

We now prove the assertion of Gödel's footnote 48a, that the undecidable propositions constructed in Gödel's 1931 paper become decidable whenever appropriate higher types are added, by writing down a truth definition for first-order Peano Arithmetic in second-order logic. We first introduce the concept of a truth definition in first-order logic in an extended vocabulary.[91] We then use this to obtain a second-order definition in the original vocabulary of *PA*.

An extension *T* of *PA* is said to have a *truth definition* for the language of *PA* if the following holds. The vocabulary of *T* extends the vocabulary of *PA* by a new binary predicate symbol *S*. Using Gödel's β-function we can view every number k as coding a finite sequence $((k)_0, \ldots, (k)_{n-1})$ of numbers, where we denote $\operatorname{len}(k) = n$. These numbers are used as the interpretations of the variables $x_0, \ldots, x_{n-1}$, that is, $(k)_0$ interprets x_0, and so on. We write $x \sim_i y$ if $(x)_j = (y)_j$ for all $j < \operatorname{len}(x) = \operatorname{len}(y)$ such that $j \neq i$. The functions $(x)_y$ and $x \sim_i y$ can be defined in the language of *PA* by means of the β-function. We assume *T* proves the following statements (we present the statements somewhat informally and assume there are no nested terms):

1. If x_0 is the Gödel-number of an equation $v_i = v_j$ and $i,j < \operatorname{len}(x_1)$, then $S(x_0, x_1) \leftrightarrow (x_1)_i = (x_1)_j$.
2. If x_0 is the Gödel-number of an equation $v_i + v_j = v_k$ and $i,j < \operatorname{len}(k)$, then $S(x_0, x_1) \leftrightarrow (x_1)_i + (x_1)_j = (x_1)_k$.
3. If x_0 is the Gödel-number of an equation $v_i \times v_j = v_k$ and $i,j,k < \operatorname{len}(x_1)$, then $S(x_0, x_1) \leftrightarrow (x_1)_i \times (x_1)_j = (x_1)_k$.
4. If x_0 is the Gödel-number of the negation of a formula with Gödel-number x_2, then $S(x_0, x_1) \leftrightarrow \neg S(x_2, x_1)$.
5. If x_0 is the Gödel-number of the conjunction of a formula with Gödel-number x_2 and a formula with Gödel-number x_3, then $S(x_0, x_1) \leftrightarrow S(x_2, x_1) \wedge S(x_3, x_1)$.

---

[89] In the address, Gödel only mentions OD, but one can take him to be referring to HOD in most cases.

[90] See [99]. Gödel's remarks in his 1946 lecture and elsewhere were completely prescient; however, in one or two cases his assertions were incorrect. See Gödel's *1933i* involving the decision problem for the quantifier class ∀∃∃... with identity. This was shown to be undecidable by Goldfarb [48].

[91] For extensive details on truth definitions, see [56].

6. If x_0 is the Gödel-number of the disjunction of a formula with Gödel-number x_2 and a formula with Gödel-number x_3, then $S(x_0,x_1) \leftrightarrow S(x_2,x_1) \vee S(x_3,x_1)$.

7. If x_0 is the Gödel-number of $\exists x_i \phi$, only variables $x_j, j < \text{len}(x_1)$, occur free in ϕ, and the Gödel-number of ϕ is x_2, then $S(x_0,x_1) \leftrightarrow \exists x_3(x_3 \sim_i x_1 \wedge S(x_2,x_3))$.

8. If x_0 is the Gödel-number of $\forall x_i \phi$, only variables $x_j, j < \text{len}(x_1)$, occur free in ϕ, and the Gödel-number of ϕ is x_2, then $S(x_0,x_1) \leftrightarrow \forall x_3(x_3 \sim_i x_1 \rightarrow S(x_2,x_3))$.

Let $\phi(x_0)$ be the formula $\exists x_1 S(x_0,x_1)$. This formula is a truth definition in the sense that for sentences ψ in the language of *PA*:

$$T \vdash \psi \leftrightarrow \phi(\overline{\ulcorner \psi \urcorner}). \tag{2.2}$$

An alternative to extending the vocabulary is the introduction of higher types. Namely one can write $\phi(x_0)$ in second-order logic as $\exists S(T_0(S) \wedge \exists x_1 S(x_0,x_1))$, where $T_0(S)$ consists of the conditions 1–8 above. Then $\phi(x_0)$ is in the vocabulary of *PA* but it is not first-order any more.

Note that by the Fixed Point Theorem such a truth definition $\phi(x_0)$ as in (2.2) could not exist for the entire language of T, if T is consistent. However, such truth definitions can exist if we either extend the vocabulary or extend first-order logic, or change the underlying first-order logic.

How can we use the truth definition to exhibit sentences that are true in $\mathbb{N}$, but unprovable in *PA*? We show that the sentence ψ, "I am unprovable," satisfying $T \vdash \psi \leftrightarrow \forall x \neg B(x, \ulcorner \psi \urcorner)$, which is independent from T if T is ω-consistent, is provable in T if T has a truth definition ϕ for first-order arithmetic and satisfies induction in its own vocabulary. First note that for such T, we have:

Lemma 2.4.1 $T \vdash \text{Bew}(\overline{\ulcorner \psi \urcorner}) \rightarrow \phi(\overline{\ulcorner \psi \urcorner})$.

Proof. By induction on the length of proofs. A subtle point to note is that we have to carry out the induction in the theory T in order to take care of "nonstandard" proofs as well. This is essentially as in the proof of soundness. A detailed proof is in [104]. If induction is limited to formulas in the language of *PA*, the result does not hold [19]. □

Note that this implies $T \vdash \text{Bew}(\overline{\ulcorner \psi \urcorner}) \rightarrow \psi$, whence T would go beyond first-order arithmetic. Why? Letting ψ be $0 = 1$ we obtain $T \vdash \text{Bew}(\overline{\ulcorner 0 = 1 \urcorner}) \rightarrow 0 = 1$, whence $T \vdash \neg\text{Bew}(\overline{\ulcorner 0 = 1 \urcorner})$. This would contradict Gödel's Second Incompleteness Theorem, if T was just *PA*.[92]

---

[92] See the below, the below, "The Second Incompleteness Theorem."

We now show that the lemma implies $T \vdash \psi$, where ψ is such that

$$T \vdash \psi \leftrightarrow \neg\mathrm{Bew}(\overline{\ulcorner\psi\urcorner}). \tag{2.3}$$

As above,

$$T \vdash \mathrm{Bew}(\overline{\ulcorner\psi\urcorner}) \to \psi.$$

But also by (2.3):

$$T \vdash \mathrm{Bew}(\overline{\ulcorner\psi\urcorner}) \to \neg\psi$$

Hence, by propositional logic,

$$T \vdash \neg\mathrm{Bew}(\overline{\ulcorner\psi\urcorner})$$

Hence, by (2.3) $T \vdash \psi$.

Set theory. If the Incompleteness Theorem is proved for set theory, for example, *ZFC*, there is yet another way to extend the theory so that it proves the undecidable statement *Con(ZFC)*.[93] Such an extension of *ZFC* is found by adding the axiom stating the existence of a strongly inaccessible cardinal κ.[94] Sets of rank smaller than κ form then a model V_κ of *ZFC*, that is, *Con(ZFC)* becomes provable. There is also a truth definition for V_κ in $V_{\kappa+\omega}$ so the independent statement "I am unprovable (in *ZFC*)" becomes provable in the new theory. Gödel himself refers (vaguely) to this in his footnote 48a and more explicitly in his 1934 lectures: "It can be shown that it is decidable in the next higher type, but there is another such statement which is not decidable even in that type, but which is decidable by going into the next higher type; *and so on [including transfinite iterations describable in set theory, such as occur, e.g., in the higher axioms of infinity]*."[95]

2.4.2 Section 3 of 1931

In Gödel's section 3 of the paper, devoted to consequences of Theorem VI, Gödel shows that the undecidable sentence can be taken to be *arithmetical* (Theorem VIII). That is, the form of the undecidable sentence can be taken to be that of a polynomial equation with coefficients in the natural numbers, with a quantifier prefix consisting of a block of alternating quantifiers. Gödel's original proof was set in a type-theoretic and not an arithmetic framework,

---

[93] *Con(ZFC)* is the sentence $\neg\mathrm{Bew}(\overline{\ulcorner 0 = 1 \urcorner})$, where Bew is written for *ZFC* rather than for *PA*.

[94] A cardinal is strongly inaccessible if it is regular and strong limit.

[95] [42], p. 367.

so the Theorem VIII is important and meaningful, giving the first "mathematical" proof of the First Incompleteness Theorem.[96] If Gödel had set his theorem not in type theory but in a first-order formulation of Peano Arithmetic, Theorem VIII would of course be unnecessary, as, trivially, *everything* stated in Peano Arithmetic is arithmetic.[97] Gödel needed alternating quantifiers, as the groundbreaking MRDP theorem (so-called) stating that the Σ_1 or recursively enumerable (r.e.) sets are of *Diophantine* form, that is, of the form $\exists \vec{x}(P(\vec{x}, y) = Q(\vec{x}, y))$, where $P(\vec{x}, y), Q(\vec{x}, y)$ are polynomials with natural number coefficients, was proved only much later in 1970 by Matiyasevich on the basis of papers by Robinson, Davis, and Putnam, giving a solution to Hilbert's Tenth Problem.[98]

Gödel ends this section with his important Theorems IX and X. Theorem IX says that the undecidable sentence of Theorem VI can be taken to be first-order, recalling that Gödel's theorem VI was stated for the simple theory of types. Theorem X, which implies Theorem IX, revisits the concept of truth in the standard model. Footnote 55 here reads, helpfully: "In 1930 I showed that every formula of the restricted functional calculus either can be proved to be valid or has a counterexample. However, by Theorem IX the existence of this counterexample is not always provable (in the formal systems we have been considering)." Theorems IX and X, quoting from *1931*, are as follows:

Theorem 2.4.2 (Theorem IX) *In any of the formal systems mentioned in Theorem V, there are undecidable problems of the restricted functional calculus (that is, formulas of the restricted functional calculus [i.e., first-order predicate calculus] for which neither validity nor the existence of a counterexample is provable).*

Theorem 2.4.3 (Theorem X) *Every problem of the form $\forall x F(x)$ (with recursive F) can be reduced to the question whether a certain formula of the restricted functional calculus is satisfiable (that is, for every recursive F, we can find a formula of the restricted functional calculus that is satisfiable if and only if $\forall x F(x)$ is true).*

---

[96] See below, "Mathematical Completeness," for others.

[97] Gödel would say later that he was spurred to express his undecidable sentence in Diophantine form by von Neumann, during a conversation between the two that took place shortly after Gödel's momentous announcement in Königsberg. See [136], pp. 83-84.

[98] See Davis [11], Robinson [112], Davis and Putnam [15], Davis, Putnam, and Robinson [16], and Matiyasevic [98]. In Gödel's 1934 Princeton Lectures he shows in his Theorem II that the undecidable sentence exhibited in his 1931 paper can be taken to be "almost Diophantine," i.e., of "class A," which is defined as the class of sentences of the form $(\forall a_1, \ldots, a_m)(\exists x_1, \ldots, x_n)D$ where D is a Diophantine equation with natural number coefficients.

By "problem of the form $\forall x F(x)$" Gödel means here the problem of whether $\mathbb{N} \models \forall x F(x)$, and by "recursive" Gödel means as usual primitive recursive. Note that if Theorem X holds, then every problem of Σ_1 form can be reduced to the validity of the formula in question. By Gödel's Completeness Theorem, this is same as reducing the question whether a Σ_1 formula holds in $\mathbb{N}$ to its provability. This brings us to the *Entscheidungsproblem*, or the Decision Problem, so-called, which, as Herbrand would remark in 1929, "...is the most important of those, which exist at present in mathematics."[99] Gödel did not solve it but he easily could have, as some have suggested,[100] modulo accepting Church's Thesis and modulo accepting the concept of truth in $\mathbb{N}$.

2.4.3 Gödel and the Entscheidungsproblem

Before taking up the *Entscheidungsproblem*, we first fix our terminology; as we noted, Gödel uses the term "recursive" for what is now known as "primitive recursive" in his 1931 paper. In his 1934 lectures, Gödel introduces the term "general recursive," which is now known as "partial recursive" or, equivalently, "computable." A partial recursive (or, equivalently, computable) function that happens to be total is referred to by some as "recursive" and we adopt this terminology here. A set that is the range of a partial recursive function is known as recursively enumerable (r.e.). It is a basic fact that the r.e. sets are definable by a Σ_1 formula.

Now to the *Entscheidungsproblem*. Formulated in its standard form in Hilbert and Ackermann's 1928 [60], it asks whether there is an algorithm for deciding validity for first-order logic, that is, if there is an algorithm that decides in a yes-or-no manner for any first-order statement P whether it is valid or not. Gödel's Completeness Theorem equates first-order validity with the existence of a finite proof, so the *Entscheidungsproblem* is equivalent to the question whether, for any recursively axiomatized first-order theory, there is an algorithm for deciding whether a first-order statement in the language of the theory follows from the axioms. Put another way, given that the provability predicate for, for example, first-order Peano Arithmetic is Σ_1 (or recursively enumerable, i.e., r.e.), the *Entscheidungsproblem* asks whether the provability predicate for, for example, first-order Peano is not only r.e. but recursive.

The unsolvability of the Decision Problem, or the *Entscheidungsproblem*, was established independently by Church [10] and Turing [127] in 1936, using conceptually distinct methods. The unsolvability follows immediately from the existence of an r.e. non-recursive set; if first-order provability were recursive,

---

[99] [59], p. 42.
[100] Notably Kripke in his recent paper [82].

then every Σ_1 problem would be recursive.[101] But we know after 1936 that this is not so, there are r.e. nonrecursive predicates, that is, r.e. sets whose characteristic function is not total recursive.[102] Note the implicit use of *Church's Thesis* here; the notion of "algorithm" at issue in the *Entscheidungsproblem* is adequately represented by the mathematical notion of "recursive."

Many logicians have remarked on the close relationship between the *Entscheidungsproblem* and incompleteness, notably Gandy. "Thus Gödel's result," as Gandy would write in his brilliant (and brilliantly titled) survey paper "The confluence of ideas in 1936" [38], "meant that it was almost inconceivable that the *Entscheidungsproblem* should be decidable: a solution could, so to speak, only work by magic."[103] What Gandy means here, presumably, is that a solution to the *Entscheidungsproblem* would deliver an algorithm that always halts; however, this fact could not be *proved*.

Does Gödel's *1931* actually solve the *Entscheidungsproblem*? Kripke addresses the point at length in his recent [82], making in it the following claim: Gandy's above-quoted remark is "much too weak," as the unsolvability of the *Entscheidungsproblem* is a *corollary* of Gödel's *1931* paper, in particular of Theorem IX:

> Gödel's Theorem IX clearly directly implies Turing's result that the *Entscheidungsproblem* is not decidable on one of his machines, since we can simply add an axiomatization of the operation of the machine to his basic system.

The argument, roughly, is as follows. We first adopt Kripke's (in his terminology) "logical" view of computation, namely that computation should be regarded as a special form of mathematical argument:

> My main point is this: a computation is a special form of mathematical argument. One is given a set of instructions, and the steps in the computation are supposed to follow – follow deductively – from the instructions as given. *So a computation is just another mathematical deduction, albeit one of a very specialized form.* In particular, the conclusion of the argument follows from the instructions as given and perhaps some well-known and not explicitly stated mathematical premises. I will assume that the computation is a deductive argument from a finite number of instructions, in analogy to Turing's emphasis on our finite capacity. It is in this sense, namely that I am regarding

---

[101] This relies on Σ_1-completeness of *PA*, namely the fact that if a Σ_1 formula holds in $\mathbb{N}$, i.e., if there is a natural number witness n to a Σ_1 formula, this is actually provable in *PA*. See, for example, [66], section 2.2.

[102] See Kleene [74], reprinted in Davis's [12]. This proves what Church called the second form of the *Entscheidungsproblem*. See Davis's [12], p. 109, and Kleene's introduction in [42], p. 136.

[103] [38], p. 63.

computation as a special form of deduction, that I am saying I am advocating a logical orientation to the problem ... I have thus proposed that derivability from a finite set of instructions statable in a first-order mathematical language be taken to be the basic technical concept of computability.[104]

The second ingredient Kripke relies on for his claim that the negative solution of the *Entscheidungsproblem* is a corollary of Gödel's Theorem IX is what he calls "Hilbert's Thesis," namely the idea that "the steps of any mathematical argument can be given in a language based on first-order logic (with identity)."[105] Kripke will use Hilbert's Thesis together with Gödel's Completeness Theorem to infer that any *valid* computation, if viewed as a valid deduction, is provable in any of the standard first-order formal systems.

Now to Gödel's system we can add the rules governing the operation of the algorithm that purportedly solves the *Entscheidungsproblem*, which are statable in a first-order language, as above. Then in this enhanced system S', any first-order proposition is decided, contradicting Gödel's Theorem IX.

We reconstruct Kripke's actual argument as follows. Suppose the algorithm α solves the *Entscheidungsproblem*. Let Σ be strong enough both to prove Gödel's Theorem X and to formalize validity. (E.g., Σ can be ZF^-, i.e., the theory ZF without the power set axiom.) Applying Kripke's two principles "computability as a form of deduction" and Hilbert's Thesis, let $A(x)$ say that the algorithm α halts and says that x is valid. Then for all ψ, $\Sigma \vdash A(\psi)$ or $\Sigma \vdash \neg A(\psi)$, because α always gives an answer. We may assume Σ includes $\forall x(A(x) \equiv Val(x))$. By Gödel's Theorem IX, together with the First Incompleteness Theorem, there is ϕ_Σ such that ϕ_Σ is satisfiable (has a model) but $\Sigma \nvdash$ "ϕ_Σ is satisfiable". Then:

- $\Sigma \nvdash Sat(\phi_\Sigma)$, by the above. ($\Sigma$ can express $Sat(x)$, i.e. that x is satisfiable.)
- $\Sigma \nvdash \neg Val(\neg\phi_\Sigma)$, by logic. ($\Sigma$ can express $Val(x)$, i.e. that x is valid.)
- $\Sigma \nvdash \neg A(\neg\phi_\Sigma)$, by logic.
- $\Sigma \vdash A(\neg\phi_\Sigma)$, because α gives always an answer.
- $\Sigma \vdash Val(\neg\phi_\Sigma)$, a contradiction with the assumption that ϕ_Σ is satisfiable.

Why didn't Gödel supply this easy argument, once the Incompleteness Theorems were in place? Kripke explains this by reverting to Gödel's hesitation to accept Church's Thesis prior to 1936, which is well known.[106] But there is also the issue of truth:

---

[104] [82], pp. 80–82.

[105] [82], p. 81.

[106] For discussion of Gödel's hesitation to accept Church's Thesis prior to 1936 see [68]. Church's Thesis, as originally suggested by Church in 1934, identified effective calculability with λ-calculability, and then with Herbrand-Gödel calculability, after the equivalence between the two was established. Nowadays Church's Thesis is identified with the broader proposition

why didn't Gödel . . . regard Theorem IX as such a proof? One problem in the argument I have given that Theorem IX is such a proof is its free use of the notion of truth, and locating the trouble in one extra axiom that must be false. However, it seems very unlikely that Gödel, at least, would have regarded that as a questionable part of the argument. What seems most likely lacking is an appropriate analog of Church's thesis.[107]

We saw that Gödel went to great trouble to excise semantic notions from the proof of the First Incompleteness Theorem. Presumably the same set of pressures would have operated on Gödel in the case of the *Entscheidungsproblem*. So we differ with Kripke on this point. As for Church's Thesis, it is well known that Gödel did not accept that thesis prior to Turing's work,[108] so Kripke is entirely correct on this score.

2.5 Computability

The First Incompleteness Theorem is commonly phrased as follows. There is a mathematical statement G that is true but unprovable. More precisely, given any consistent formal system T strong enough to code the basic properties of finite sequences there is a statement that is true in the natural numbers but unprovable in T. One may ask, why not add G as an axiom? As we know, the resulting system is still incomplete. One may *then* ask, why not add all statements true in the natural numbers as axioms? In that case we do capture all the truths of arithmetic, so this system is complete in that sense. However it is not *effective*, that is, the resulting theory is not recursively axiomatizable. What saves the First Incompleteness Theorem from triviality, then – what gives the First Incompleteness Theorem its *power* – is the concept of effectivity.

Thus if the First Incompleteness Theorem is thought of as saying that formal systems of a certain very basic kind, which is to say effective and strong enough in the above sense, cannot capture all arithmetic truths, understanding the meaning of the theorem, and particularly gaining clarity on its *scope*, depends on a having a clear notion, first, of the notion of "effective," and, second, of the notion of "formal system." As for the notion of truth that appears prominently here, we noted its excision from the theorem. Interestingly enough, unlike the notions of effectivity and of formal system, providing an explication of truth was not considered to be a piece of unfinished business by Gödel at this point. And indeed as the years went on, Gödel would simply adopt the notion

---

that human effective calculability is adequately represented by the Turing Machine model of computability, or any of its equivalents.

[107] [82], p. 88.

[108] We elaborate on this point in Section 2.5.

of truth as a primitive in his writings, Gödel's 1946 Princeton Bicentennial Lecture being a prime example.[109]

As it turns out, Turing's modeling of the notion "humanly effectively calculable" via his Machines definitively solved *both* problems for Gödel: the problem of clarifying the concept of "formal system" and the problem of adequacy with respect to the concept of "human effectively computable." For Gödel, the concept of formal system would become identical with that of a Turing Machine. As he would later say: "In my opinion the term 'formal system' or 'formalism' should never be used for anything but this notion [i.e., a mechanical procedure in the sense of the Turing Machine]."[110]

We take a moment to explain this development. As we noted, the First Incompleteness Theorem was proved quite early in terms of the development of computability theory. As various models of computability began to emerge in the 1930s, the 1934 Herbrand–Gödel notion of general recursiveness among them, the question arose whether the various models of computable function that had emerged prior to 1936 were *adequate* for the notion of "humanly effectively computable." Gödel was not convinced, saying of the Herbrand–Gödel recursive functions – the model of computation used in his 1934 lectures cited above – that it was not clear that all recursions were covered by the model, in spite of the fact that the Herbrand–Gödel recursive functions had been shown to be equivalent to the other models of computation that were known at the time.[111] In particular Herbrand and Gödel had agreed in their correspondence that the concept of finite computation was itself "undefinable," a view Gödel held through 1934 (and beyond), when he wrote the oft-quoted footnote 3 to the lecture notes of his Princeton lectures:

> The converse seems to be true if, besides recursions according to the scheme (2), recursions of other forms (e.g. with respect to two variables simultaneously) are admitted. This cannot be proved, since the notion of finite computation is not defined, but serves as a heuristic principle.[112]

Another stream of ideas generated by the Incompleteness Theorems concern the concept of a *formal system*. The notion seems to be clearly defined, on

---

[109] But see Gödel's notes on Russell's Multiple Relation Theory of truth (MRT), made during the preparation of his 1944 paper "On Russell's mathematical logic." The notes are in volumes IX and X of the so-called Max Phil notebooks. Floyd and Kanamori [27] provide an extensive analysis of Gödel and the MRT.

[110] [42], p. 195.

[111] See also Kleene's remarks in [42], p. 347, to the effect that Gödel was not convinced of Church's Thesis in 1934.

[112] The claim, the converse of which is being considered here, is that functions computable by a finite procedure are recursive in the sense given in the lectures [42], p. 348.

its face – but how do we know that the notion of "formal system" does not admit pathological counterexamples? Mathematicians are familiar with this phenomenon; for example, in the nineteenth century the notion of continuity was thought to be well understood; however, Weierstrass's definition of "continuous function" was shown to admit pathological counterexamples in the form of space-filling or Peano curves (i.e., "dust").

Second, how do we know that the formal systems at hand are broad enough to formalize everything of interest? Is it possible that there are finitary proofs that are not formalizable in the systems in question? Gödel is cautious on this point in his 1931 paper:

> For this [formalist] viewpoint presupposes only the existence of a consistency proof in which nothing but finitary means of proof is used, and it is conceivable that there exist finitary proofs that cannot be expressed in the formalism of P (or of M and A).[113]

The issue is clearly a pressing one, because without a precise and adequate definition of the concept of formal system, it is not clear what the scope of the Incompleteness Theorem should be.

By 1935, Gödel's reflections on computability in the higher-order context began to point toward the possibility of a definitive notion of formal system. Nevertheless, an absolute definition, in Gödel's terminology, of effective computability was still missing at that point. As Gödel wrote to Kreisel in 1965:

> That my [incompleteness] results were valid for all possible formal systems began to be plausible for me (that is since 1935) only because of the Remark printed on p. 83 of "The Undecidable" ...But I was completely convinced only by Turing's paper.[114]

In 1936 Turing's model of computability, the Turing Machine as it is now known, solved *both* problems for Gödel, and also for the wider logical community: the problem of adequacy for the concept "humanly effectively computable" as well as the problem of the generality of the First Incompleteness Theorem. This turns on having a correct and fully adequate definition of the concept of "formal system." We cited Gödel's 1965 letter to Kreisel above;

---

[113] [42], p. 195. P is a variant of *Principia mathematica*.

[114] Quoted in Sieg [117], in turn quoting from an unpublished manuscript of Odifreddi, p. 65. Gödel's "Remark" is contained in the addendum to the 1936 abstract "On the lengths of proofs": "It can, moreover, be shown that a function computable in one of the [higher-order] systems S_i, or even in a system of transfinite order, is computable already in S_1. Thus the notion 'computable' is *in a certain sense* 'absolute', while almost all metamathematical notions otherwise known (for example, provable, definable, and so on) quite essentially depend on the system adopted." "On the length of proofs," [42], p. 399. Emphasis added.

other evidence of this in the record is to be found in the 1965 publication of Gödel's 1934 Princeton Lectures, which include the following postscriptum, added in 1964:

> In consequence of later advances, in particular of the fact that, due to A. M. Turing's work, a precise and unquestionably adequate definition of the general concept of formal system can now be given, the existence of undecidable arithmetical propositions and the non-demonstrability of the consistency of a system in the same system can now be proved rigorously for every consistent formal system containing a certain amount of finitary number theory.
>
> Turing's work gives an analysis of the concept of "mechanical procedure" (alias algorithm or computation procedure or "finite combinatorial procedure"). This concept is shown to be equivalent with that of a "Turing machine." A formal system can simply be defined to be any mechanical procedure for producing formulas, called provable formulas. For any formal system in this sense there exists one in the [usual] sense that has the same provable formulas (and likewise vice versa), provided the term "finite procedure" occurring on page 346 is understood to mean "mechanical procedure." This meaning, however, is required by the concept of formal system, whose essence it is that reasoning is completely replaced by mechanical operations on formulas.[115]

It is not entirely obvious why regarding a formal system as a machine (in Turing's sense) should have solved the scope problem for Gödel. Indeed, to this day, the claim that Gödel relies on here, that Turing's model captures entirely the concept of human effectivity, and more broadly the status of Church's Thesis itself, remains somewhat controversial. In [72] it is argued that underlying Gödel's move here, that is, seeing the scope problem as solved by the Turing analysis of computable function, is a particular view of natural language, to wit: giving a formalism-independent or formalism-free presentation of the concept of "formal system," a view coming through very clearly also in Tarski's work

---

[115] [42], p. 369. These are Gödel's later remarks but contemporary references on Gödel's gloss on Turing's work with regard to the notion of formal system would include the text *193?*, [45] dating presumably from the years 1936–1939. In the text, Gödel gives a perspicuous presentation of the Herbrand–Gödel equational calculus. He also improves the result of the 1934 lectures, that undecidable sentences for the formal theories in question can be given in the form of Diophantine equations, by showing that the Diophantine equations in question are limited in degree and in the number of variables (while not actually computing the bound). His view of Turing's work at the time:

> When I first published my paper about undecidable propositions the result could not be pronounced in this generality, because for the notions of mechanical procedure and of formal system no mathematically satisfactory definition had been given at the time. This gap has since been filled by Herbrand, Church and Turing. The essential point is to define what a procedure is. Then the notion of formal system follows easily ...

[45], p. 166.

(albeit stated in very different terms), is to reach a perfect endpoint in the analysis (of the concept of "formal system").

2.5.1 Proving the First Incompleteness Theorem from the Existence of a Noncomputable Set

In a 2006 paper [14] Davis suggests that while "a whiff of paradox might hang over the matter" of the proof of the First Incompleteness Theorem, the perspective of computability reveals the fundamentality of that theorem. As evidence Davis reminds us of what was mentioned in our discussion of Gödel and the *Entscheidungsproblem*, namely that the First Incompleteness Theorem also follows easily from the existence of an r.e. nonrecursive set.

We prove this now. Suppose S is an r.e. nonrecursive set. Such sets are easy to find, for example, from the Halting Problem. Let $R(x,y)$ be a p.r. relation such that

$$n \in S \iff \exists y R(n,y),$$

and suppose T is a consistent recursively axiomatized theory in which primitive recursive predicates can be strongly represented.

Theorem 2.5.1 *There is n such that $\forall x \neg R(n,x)$ is true but unprovable from T.*

Proof. Suppose all true $\forall x \neg R(n,x)$ are provable in T. Note that if $n \in S$, then $R(n,m)$ for some m, whence $T \vdash R(\overline{n},\overline{m})$, and further $T \vdash \neg\forall x \neg R(\overline{n},x)$. Thus for each n, according to whether $n \notin S$ or $n \in S$, we have either $T \vdash \forall x \neg R(\overline{n},x)$ or $T \vdash \neg\forall x \neg R(\overline{n},x)$, but not both because T is consistent. Now we can decide $n \in S$ by starting to list the theorems of T and waiting to see which of $\forall x \neg R(\overline{n},x)$ and $\neg\forall x \neg R(\overline{n},x)$ appears, knowing that one will. Thus S is recursive, a contradiction. □

2.6 The Fixed Point Theorem from the Computability Point of View

A final note on the Fixed Point Theorem. The powerful resonance between incompleteness and computability comes out particularly strongly in the case of this theorem. In the hands of computability theorists, the theorem emerges in the form of the *Second Recursion Theorem*, due to Kleene.[116] The theorem depends on two facts: first, that every partial recursive function f has an index relative to an enumeration of all partial recursive functions ϕ_e; second, the so-called *s-m-n* theorem, which says that there is a total recursive function $s(z,\vec{y})$

---

[116] [75].

such that for all indices e: $\phi_e(\vec{y},\vec{x}) = \phi_{s(e,\vec{y})}(\vec{x})$. The *s-m-n* theorem can be easily proved directly; it also follows by a particularly easy application of Church's Thesis, in that one infers the intuitive computability of the function $\phi_{s(e,\vec{y})}(\vec{x})$ from the computability of the function ϕ_e as follows: "given $e,\vec{y},\vec{x}$, go to the e-th computable function and evaluate it on the inputs $\vec{y},\vec{x}$." With these two facts in place we can now state and prove the Second Recursion Theorem:

Theorem 2.6.1 *Let $f(e,\vec{y},\vec{x})$ be an $m + n + 1$-ary computable function. Then there is a total m-ary computable function $g(\vec{y})$ such that*

$$\phi_{g(\vec{y})}(\vec{x}) = f(g(\vec{y}),\vec{y},\vec{x}), \vec{y} \in \mathbb{N}^m, \vec{x} \in \mathbb{N}^n.$$

The proof is a one-liner:

Proof. Let e be such that $\phi_e(t,\vec{y},\vec{x}) = f(s(t,t,\vec{y}),\vec{y},\vec{x})$ and let $g(\vec{y}) = s(e,e,\vec{y})$. $\square$

In his paper "Kleene's amazing Second Recursion Theorem" [101] Moschovakis wonders at the fact that a theorem with such a simple proof should have such a wide range of significant applications, serving as it does as a fundamental step in justifying "powerful, self-referential definitions." He also sees it as enabling a "pure" form of self-reference, to wit: letting $m = n = 0$ we get:

$$\phi_g() = f(g).$$

Why "pure"? Ordinarily this just indicates that the equation has no free variables in it. But a second sense of purity is surely in play; the general Fixed Point Theorem for an appropriate theory T gives fixed points for any property expressible in the language of the theory T. Here with the Second Recursion Theorem the notion of property is greatly sharpened; fixed points are obtained for computable functions, rather than for arbitrary T-expressible properties; and the fixed point itself has the form of an index of a computable function, relative to some fixed enumeration of these.

Here is the Fixed Point Theorem stripped to its essentials – the final word, as it were.

THE SECOND INCOMPLETENESS THEOREM
3 The Unprovability of Consistency

Gödel's First Incompleteness Theorem exhibits a true but unprovable statement, whose negation is also unprovable. The *Second* Incompleteness Theorem exhibits an independent statement of a specific kind, namely the – or, more precisely, a – consistency statement for the theory in question, as the consistency of a theory can be stated in many different ways. This launches a second attack on the Hilbert Program, which in addition to completeness had asked for a finitary, internal consistency proof for analysis.[117]

Gödel's Second Incompleteness Theorem states that for the theories in question, consistency cannot be proved internally – not for analysis, and not even for Peano Arithmetic (and indeed as we know now, not for much weaker systems). The proof is, in a sense, a one-liner – while at the same time it is a coding nightmare, or at least it was in 1930.

To see that the proof is a one-liner, recall that Gödel's First Incompleteness Theorem states that there are sentences that are true in the natural numbers, but that are unprovable in the theory S in which Gödel worked, provided the theory is consistent. The insight here is that the reasoning involved in the proof of the First Incompleteness Theorem does not go beyond the reasoning licensed by S, and therefore the proof of the First Incompleteness Theorem can be formalized in S. The theorem is as follows, with *PA* as the base theory as usual:

Theorem 3.0.1 (Theorem XI) *For* Bew(x) *as in Theorem VI, let Con(PA) be the following sentence in the language of PA:* ¬Bew($\overline{\ulcorner 0 = 1 \urcorner}$). *Then if PA is consistent, Con(PA) is not provable in PA.*

Proof. Let ϕ be a fixed point of the predicate ¬Bew(x) of Theorem VI, that is,

$$PA \vdash \phi \leftrightarrow \neg\text{Bew}(\overline{\ulcorner \phi \urcorner}).$$

Formalizing the proof of the First Incompleteness Theorem in *PA* yields

$$PA \vdash Bew(\overline{\ulcorner \phi \urcorner}) \rightarrow \neg Con(PA), \tag{3.1}$$

and thus by the definition of ϕ,

$$PA \vdash Con(PA) \rightarrow \phi.$$

Since $PA \nvdash \phi$, it must be that $PA \nvdash Con(PA)$. $\qquad\square$

Note that ω-consistency is not needed in the proof of Gödel's Second Incompleteness Theorem. Note also that if we assume ω-consistency, then also ¬$Con(PA)$ is unprovable.

The formalization step, that is, the work involved in expressing 3.1, was omitted in *1931*, whose last line is: "In that paper [i.e., part II of Gödel's *1931*], also, the proof of Theorem XI, only sketched here, will be given in detail." As it turns out, Gödel never wrote what was to be part II of *1931*, as the sketch of the Second Incompleteness Theorem given in part I was enough to convince

---

[117] For the desiderata of the program see, e.g., Hilbert's [64], p. 540. We take up the impact of the Incompleteness Theorems on the Hilbert Program below in Section 4.4.

the logicians of the time of its validity. It must be said that standards of rigor shift over time, so nowadays perhaps one would have had to say more than Gödel does in his *1931*.[118] As Kleene put it: "Certainly the idea of the argument for Theorem XI (consistency) was very convincing; but it turned out that the execution of the details required somewhat more work and care than had been anticipated."[119] Eventually a complete proof of the Second Incompleteness Theorem was given by Hilbert and Bernays in some 60 pages in their 1939 book [62]. A much more compact treatment of the theorem was given by Löb in his 1955 paper [89], and by now there are many, many different proofs of the Second Incompleteness Theorem: model-theoretic proofs of various kinds as well as many others, for example, involving Kolmogorov complexity due to Chaitin, and proofs based on remarkable cardinals due to Friedman. There is even a proof of the Second Incompleteness Theorem based on the surprise examination paradox, due to Kritchman and Raz [84].

Before turning to Löb's Theorem, which places adequacy conditions on the provability predicate of the theory, we recount here an interesting episode surrounding the Second Incompleteness Theorem. Immediately after Gödel's announcement of the First Incompleteness Theorem at the September 1930 Königsberg meeting, von Neumann and Gödel spoke about the result. A few months after the Königsberg meeting (on November 20), von Neumann wrote Gödel that using the methods of the First Incompleteness Theorem, one can derive the unprovability of consistency. Gödel replied that he had done this, and indeed Gödel had sent an abstract to the Vienna Academy (the text *1930b* on [42]) on October 30, of both the First and Second Incompleteness Theorems, the abstract having been presented to the Vienna Academy of Sciences by Hans Hahn on October 23. A few more letters were exchanged, at the end of which von Neumann wrote, "Many thanks for your letter and your reprint. As you have established the theorem on the unprovability of consistency as a natural continuation and deepening of your earlier results, I clearly won't publish on this subject."[120] Looking back, one may raise the question whether the Second Incompleteness Theorem should not be credited to Gödel and von Neumann jointly, even so that there is a time gap of at least a month, and very likely a number of months. At the end of the day it is best in such matters to leave the decision on authorship to the figures involved – after all, they are the only ones who know all the facts.

---

[118] On the other hand published mathematical papers today are full of statements that a theorem can be proved, accompanied by a proof sketch.

[119] [42], p. 137.

[120] [47], p. 339.

4 Löb Conditions and Adequacy

Löb [89] introduced, as a modification of conditions given in Hilbert and Bernays's 1939 publication [62], conditions for the provability predicate to satisfy in order that the Second Incompleteness Theorem holds. The conditions are as follows:

I If $PA \vdash \phi$, then $PA \vdash \mathrm{Bew}(\overline{\ulcorner\phi\urcorner})$.

II $PA \vdash \mathrm{Bew}(\overline{\ulcorner\phi \to \psi\urcorner}) \to (\overline{\mathrm{Bew}(\overline{\ulcorner\phi\urcorner}) \to \mathrm{Bew}(\ulcorner\psi\urcorner)})$.

III $PA \vdash \mathrm{Bew}(\overline{\ulcorner\phi\urcorner}) \to \mathrm{Bew}(\ulcorner\mathrm{Bew}(\overline{\ulcorner\phi\urcorner})\urcorner)$.

Löb also proved a strengthening of the Second Incompleteness Theorem:

Theorem 4.0.1 *If $PA \vdash \mathrm{Bew}(\overline{\ulcorner\phi\urcorner}) \to \phi$, then $PA \vdash \phi$.*

The Second Incompleteness Theorem now follows from the above theorem: Assume $PA \nvdash \bot$. Then by the Theorem, $PA \nvdash \mathrm{Bew}(\overline{\ulcorner\bot\urcorner}) \to \bot$, that is, $PA \nvdash \neg\mathrm{Bew}(\overline{\ulcorner\bot\urcorner})$.

The Löb conditions are thought to divide "legitimate" provability predicates from deviant ones.[121] For, as Mostowski points out in [103], if we take $B(x,y)$ to represent as usual the predicate "x codes a proof of the formula with Gödel number y," and the consistency of arithmetic to be expressed by the formula $\forall x \neg B(x, \overline{\ulcorner 0 = 1\urcorner})$, then we can devise a "deviant" provability predicate:

$$B'(x,y) \equiv B(x,y) \wedge \neg B(x, \overline{\ulcorner 0 = 1\urcorner}).$$

Mostowski's point is that we could have taken this deviant formula to represent provability:

Lemma 4.0.2 *If PA is consistent, then $B'(x,y)$ strongly represents "x codes a proof of y".*

Proof. Suppose n codes a proof of a formula with Gödel number m. Then $PA \vdash B(\overline{n},\overline{m})$. Since PA is assumed to be consistent, $m \neq \ulcorner 0 = 1\urcorner$. Hence, $PA \vdash \neg B(\overline{n}, \overline{\ulcorner 0 = 1\urcorner})$. Thus, $PA \vdash B'(\overline{n},\overline{m})$. The proof is similar in the case that n does not code a proof of a formula with Gödel number m. $\square$

If we had taken this deviant formula to represent provability, the consistency of PA would be written as $\forall x \neg \mathrm{Bew}'(x, \overline{\ulcorner 0 = 1\urcorner})$. But then the consistency of PA would be provable in PA:

Lemma 4.0.3 $PA \vdash \forall x \neg B'(x, \overline{\ulcorner 0 = 1\urcorner})$.

---

[121] They should be thought of as necessary but not sufficient conditions for "legitimate" provability predicates.

Proof. Trivially, $\neg B'(x, \overline{\ulcorner 0 = 1 \urcorner})$ is equivalent to the tautology

$$\neg B(x, \overline{\ulcorner 0 = 1 \urcorner}) \vee B(x, \overline{\ulcorner 0 = 1 \urcorner})$$

and therefore provable in *PA* (and even without *PA*). Hence, again trivially

$$PA \vdash \forall x \neg B'(x, \overline{\ulcorner 0 = 1 \urcorner}). \qquad \Box$$

Thus for some provability predicates the consistency *is* provable, raising the question whether there is some choice for the provability predicate, smarter than the above B', for which consistency is suddenly provable. Löb's conditions show that consistency is unprovable for *any* provability predicate that satisfies his conditions, as we argued after Theorem 4.0.1.[122] But that did not end the discussion of deviance, and indeed other forms of deviance soon began to emerge.

It should be noted that it is a nontrivial task to demonstrate that particular provability predicates satisfy the Löb conditions.

4.1 Axiomatizations

As part of the provability predicate one has to (strongly) represent the set of Gödel numbers of the axioms. There are canonical representations, such as those Gödel used. But what if we use some other representation – is the Second Incompleteness Theorem still valid? In Feferman's landmark paper "Arithmetization of metamathematics in a general setting" [20] he exhibits representations of the axioms of the theory for which the associated consistency statement is provable.

Feferman then defines what a "recursively enumerable" representation of the axioms would look like and then defines what an "r.e." representation of the axioms in this sense would look like. He then proves that the Second Incompleteness Theorem holds for such representations.

4.2 Numbering

As an essential part of the proof of the Second Incompleteness Theorem one has to devise a Gödel numbering of the symbols and expressions of *PA*. There is the ordinary Gödel numbering used by Gödel, but what if we use some other Gödel numbering? Is the Second Incompleteness Theorem still valid? In his [49], Grabmayr showed that one can exhibit Gödel numberings that violate the Second Incompleteness Theorem, that is, for which the associated consistency statement is provable in *PA*. He uses even numbers to code provable sentences

---

[122] See [85] for a recent survey.

and odd numbers to code all the rest, and the resulting provability predicate still satisfies the Löb conditions.[123]

Grabmayr then defines the concept of "admissible" Gödel numbering. Note that one cannot just stipulate that the set of Gödel numbers of syntactic strings is, for example, an r.e. set, because the expressions are not themselves natural numbers. Grabmayr overcomes this and defines what an "admissible" numbering would look like; he then proves that the Second Incompleteness Theorem holds for such numberings. He also does the same for notation systems, that is, he exhibits deviant notation systems violating the Second Incompleteness Theorem.

The literature on deviance is relatively substantial and the philosophical issues are deep. The problem is not that deviance exists; it is rather that, as in the case of computability, where the problem is also acute, it is difficult to separate the deviant from the nondeviant.

4.3 Consistency is Provable with Extra Assumptions

4.3.1 Gentzen

Peano Arithmetic includes among its axioms an induction schema for inductive proofs on the canonical well-order of the natural numbers. In fact induction can also be proved for more complicated well-orderings. For example, one can prove induction for well-orderings of type $\omega + \omega$, $\omega \cdot \omega$, and ω^ω. The limit is ϵ_0, which is the least fixed point of ordinal exponentiation or alternatively the limit of the sequence $\alpha_0 = \omega$, $\alpha_{n+1} = \omega^{\alpha_n}$, $n < \omega$. Induction over any ordinal less than ϵ_0 is provable in Peano Arithmetic. But Gentzen showed [39] that if the induction schema is assumed for well-ordering of type ϵ_0, the consistency of Peano Arithmetic is provable. Therefore, by Gödel's Second Incompleteness Theorem, induction for ϵ_0 cannot be proved in Peano Arithmetic. As opposed to the semantic proof of consistency, that is, the (trivial) proof of consistency by assuming the existence of the standard model, Gentzen's was the first proof-theoretic proof of the consistency of Peano Arithmetic.

4.3.2 Turing

Suppose T is *PA* or some other arithmetical theory for which the First Incompleteness Theorem holds. We know $T \nvdash Con(T)$. Let

$$
\begin{aligned}
T_0 &= T \\
T_{\alpha+1} &= T_\alpha \cup \{Con(T_\alpha)\} \\
T_\nu &= \bigcup_{\alpha < \nu} T_\alpha
\end{aligned}
$$

---

[123] The Fixed Point Theorem fails for this numbering.

It is not obvious how $Con(T_\alpha)$ should be defined for infinite α but we disregard this problem here. Turing [128] asked whether every number-theoretic question can be solved in some T_α. He proved the following partial result:

Theorem 4.3.1 *If ϕ is a true Π_1^0 sentence, then there is α such that $T_\alpha \vdash \phi$.*

In fact, we can choose $\alpha = \omega + 1$. Feferman [21] defines more general progressions than the above $T_0, T_1, \ldots, T_\alpha, \ldots$, based on so-called reflection principles, of which consistency statements are a special case. He showed that there is a progression of length ω^{ω^ω} such that every true arithmetical sentence is provable in some T_α.[124]

4.4 Does the Second Incompleteness Theorem Refute the Hilbert Program's Demand for an Internal Consistency Proof?

As Feferman famously pointed out in "Arithmetization of metamathematics in a general setting" [20] (following Bernays), Gödel's First Incompleteness Theorem exhibits a sentence in the language of the relevant theory that is undecided by that theory; however, the simple claim that, for example, Peano Arithmetic is incomplete does not rest on any possible meaning of the sentence in question. This is not the case with the second theorem, where the claim that any sufficiently strong theory cannot prove "its own consistency" – however that is phrased – must depend on the meaning of the consistency statement *as read by the theory*. That is, we should grant the meta-theoretical claim that a theory T cannot prove its own consistency only when there is a sentence that both T "recognizes" as a consistency statement, and that T cannot prove.

In a number of books and papers Detlefsen (among others) challenged the view that the Löb conditions identify the intensionally adequate provability predicates:

> The moral of the analyses of Bernays and Feferman, according to Mostowski, is that some metamathematical tasks (e.g., the evaluation of Hilbert's Program) call for a degree of fidelity between an arithmetical representation and the notion it represents which exceeds that which an extensionally adequate representation can guarantee. The degree of fidelity between a metamathematical notion M and the formula $\mathfrak{M}$ of T which, under arithmetization, is to represent it, is determined by the proportion of truths regarding M which are registered as theorems of T when M is "translated" as $\mathfrak{M}$. But, we must be careful to take general as well as specific truths, regarding M into the mix.

---

[124] See also Franzén's [31].

Such, at any rate, is the view of arithmetization which Mostowski urges. And it implies, or at least suggests, a corresponding defense of the Derivability Conditions. That defense, as we see it, would proceed roughly as follows: if we take as our T-theoretic representation of the notion of provability-in-T a formula satisfying the Derivability Conditions, then we will codify more truths concerning that notion as theorems of T, and hence do a better job of representing it, than we would otherwise do.

However, the cogency of this reasoning is convincingly called into question by an observation which, curiously enough, Mostowski himself makes; namely, that regardless of which formula we choose to represent the notion of provability-in-T (or such cognate notions as X's being a proof in T of Y), not all truths involving that notion will be codifiable as theorems of T.[125]

Detlefsen cites the consistency statement for T as a paradigmatic example of a truth not codifiable in T.[126]

The issue of intensional adequacy with respect to the provability predicate persists, as does a broader question: What is the finitary standpoint? The work goes on. As Hilbert and Bernays wrote in *Grundlagen der Mathematik: 1*:

> the view ...that certain recent results of Gödel show that my proof theory can't be carried out, has been shown to be erroneous. In fact that result shows only that one must exploit the finitary standpoint in a sharper way for the farther reaching consistency proofs.[127]

VARIATIONS AND PHILOSOPHICAL CONSEQUENCES
5 Other Proofs of the First and Second Theorems

The literature on the Incompleteness Theorems is overflowing with new proofs of those theorems – indeed, the reader can be assured that as they read these sentences, a logician somewhere is toiling away at producing another such proof. Giving a comprehensive survey of alternate proofs here is thus out of the question. We sample some of the early ones, chosen because they shed light on the development of certain logical interests: the search for a diagonal free proof, which begins almost immediately after the publication of *1931*; the search for a language- or even logic-free proof, under more or less Tarskian pressures (see Section 6, "Mathematical Incompleteness"); and the search for model-theoretic proofs.[128]

5.1 Kuratowski's Proof

In 1925 Kuratowski [86] proved that one cannot prove in (axiomatic) set theory that there are (strongly) inaccessible cardinals $> \omega$. The proof is as follows.

---

[125] [18], p. 103.
[126] See also Franks's [30]. For further discussion of this issue see [71].
[127] [61], p. vii.
[128] In Section 6 on mathematical incompleteness we sample some modern ones.

Suppose otherwise. Let κ be the least strongly inaccessible $> \omega$. Now V_κ is also a model of the axioms of set theory. Hence by our assumption there is an inaccessible cardinal $\lambda > \omega$ in V_κ. But then λ is really inaccessible and smaller than κ, contrary to the minimality of κ.

Models of *ZFC* of the form $(V_\kappa, \in)$ with κ strongly inaccessible are ubiquitous and well known. For the second-order *ZFC* these are, in fact, the *only* models, a fact due to Zermelo [142]. Thus the proposition "There are strongly inaccessible cardinals" can be considered a version of "There is a model of *ZFC*" and hence a form, though of course only approximately, of the statement "*ZFC* is consistent." It is in this sense that Kuratowski's result anticipates Gödel's Second Incompleteness Theorem. Kuratowski's is almost certainly the first proof of a limitative result for *ZFC*. That is, Kuratowski gives us a very natural statement that is *not* provable in *ZFC*.[129]

5.2 Robinson's Diagonal-Free Proof

In Section 2.2 we noted that in its initial form Gödel's First Incompleteness Theorem says that there must be unprovable truths, because the provables are a definable set and the truths are not, by Tarski's theorem on the undefinability of truth. In this sense Tarski's theorem implies the First Incompleteness Theorem. In fact we can obtain a diagonal-free proof of Tarski's theorem, due to Robinson [111]. Consequently, we obtain a genuinely diagonal-free proof of Gödel's First Incompleteness Theorem in its original, semantic form.

Let V be the set of Gödel numbers of true arithmetic sentences. We show that V is not a definable subset of the standard model M_0.[130] Suppose otherwise. Let $Num(x)$ be as in 2.3.2. Let $T(z)$ be a formula that defines V in M_0. Let $Len(w, t)$ strongly represent the predicate "w is the Gödel number of some formula whose length is $\leq t$." Let $Sbst(u, v, w, t)$ strongly represent "w is the Gödel number of a formula which defines a function $f(x)$ and t is the Gödel number of the sentence $Num(v) = f(Num(u))$." Now

$$M_0 \models \forall u \forall s \exists v \forall w \forall t((Len(w, s) \wedge Sbst(u, v, w, t)) \rightarrow \neg T(t)). \tag{5.1}$$

That is, "for all u and s there is v such that whichever definition of length at most s of a function $f(x)$ we take, $f(u) \neq v$." Since the number of formulas of length at most a fixed number is finite, the claim (5.1) follows trivially.

Let M be a nonstandard elementary extension of M_0 and let a be a nonstandard element in M. Let $M_0(a)$ be the intersection of all elementary submodels of

---

[129] See also Kripke [81].
[130] We usually denote M_0 by $\mathbb{N}$, but we follow here Robinson's notation.

M containing a. Since (5.1) is true (also) in $M_0(a)$, we have

$$M_0(a) \models \forall w \forall t((\text{Len}(w, Num(a)) \wedge \text{Sbst}(Num(a), Num(b), w, t)) \rightarrow \neg T(t))$$

(5.2)

for some $b \in M_0(a)$. That is, whichever definition of length $\leq a$ of a function $f(x)$ we take, the sentence $f(Num(a)) = Num(b)$ is false. There is a definition $\phi(x, y)$ for a function f such that $b = f(a)$, that is,

$$M_0(a) \models Num(b) = f(Num(a)).$$

The length of $\phi(x, y)$ is a standard number, hence smaller than a in $M_0(a)$. Let n be the Gödel number of $\phi(x, y)$. Then $\text{Len}(n, a)$ is true in $M_0(a)$ and as

$$M_0(a) \models \forall t((\text{Len}(Num(n), Num(a)) \wedge$$
$$\text{Sbst}(Num(a), Num(b), Num(n), t)) \rightarrow \neg T(t))$$

we obtain

$$M_0(a) \models \forall t(\text{Sbst}(Num(a), Num(b), Num(n), t) \rightarrow \neg T(t)),$$

(5.3)

intuitively saying that the sentence $f(a) = b$ is false. Let m be the Gödel number of the sentence $\phi(Num(a), Num(b))$. Then, by the definition of f,

$$M_0(a) \models \text{Sbst}(Num(a), Num(b), Num(n), Num(m)) \wedge T(Num(m)).$$

It follows that

$$M_0(a) \models \exists t(\text{Sbst}(Num(a), Num(b), Num(n), t) \wedge T(t)),$$

contradicting (5.3).[131]

5.3 Smullyan's Logic-Free Proof

Smullyan's remarkable proof is entirely abstract, that is to say it is entirely (formal) language- and logic-free. It is decidedly not diagonal-free, however, and indeed one would hardly expect a diagonal-free proof from this logician, who was completely enamored of diagonalization! The key concept behind Smullyan's proof is that of a representation system, about which Smullyan remarks: "The [representing] function H varies considerably from system to system, and our whole purpose is to get away from all entanglements with the formal peculiarities of particular systems, and to study representability relative to a completely arbitrary function Φ."[132] We now give Smullyan's proof.

---

[131] For a self-reference–free proof of the Second Incompleteness Theorem see also Visser's [135]. See also Visser and Halbach's [57, 58].

[132] [121], p. 39.

A *language* is a sextuple

$$\mathcal{L} = (\mathcal{E}, \mathcal{S}, \mathcal{T}, \mathcal{P}, \mathcal{H}, \Phi),$$

where

1. $\mathcal{E}$ is a countably infinite set whose elements are called the *expressions*.
2. $\mathcal{S} \subseteq \mathcal{E}$ and its elements are called the *sentences*.
3. $\mathcal{T} \subseteq \mathcal{S}$ and its elements are called the *true* sentences.
4. $\mathcal{P} \subseteq \mathcal{T}$ whose elements are called the *provable* sentences.
5. $\mathcal{H} \subseteq \mathcal{E}$ and its elements are called the *predicates*.
6. a function Φ assigns to every expression E and every natural number n an expression $E(n)$. If H is a predicate and n is a natural number, the expression $H(n)$ is always a sentence.

The point of the quintuple $\mathcal{L}$ is that it is totally abstract. All we need is an arbitrary countably infinite set $\mathcal{E}$ together with four subsets satisfying some simple inclusion and exclusion assumptions and the function Φ.

A set A of natural numbers is called *expressible* in $\mathcal{L}$ if for some predicate H of $\mathcal{L}$, for all n:

$$n \in A \iff H(n) \in \mathcal{T}.$$

Since $\mathcal{E}$ is countably infinite, there is a one-to-one function g that assigns to each expression E a natural number $g(E)$ called the *Gödel-number* of E in such a way that every number is the Gödel-number of an expression. We let E_n be that expression whose Gödel-number is n. Thus, $g(E_n) = n$. The *diagonalization* of E_n is the expression $E_n(n)$. For any n, we let $d(n)$ be the Gödel-number of $E_n(n)$. The function $d(x)$ is called the *diagonal function* of the system. For any set A of natural numbers, let A^* be defined by

$$n \in A^* \iff d(n) \in A.$$

Let $P = \{n : E_n \in \mathcal{P}\}$.

Theorem 5.3.1 *If the set* $(-P)^*$ *is expressible in* $\mathcal{L}$, *then there is a true sentence of* $\mathcal{L}$ *not provable in* $\mathcal{L}$.

Proof. Let H be a predicate that expresses $(-P)^*$ and let h be the Gödel-number of H. Let $G = H(h)$. By the choice of H and by the definition of expressibility, for any n,

$$H(n) \in \mathcal{T} \iff n \in (-P)^*.$$

Putting $n = h$ yields

$$H(h) \in \mathcal{T} \iff h \in (-P)^*.$$

Now $h \in (-P)^*$ if and only if $d(h) \in -P$ if and only if $d(h) \notin P$. But $d(h)$ is the Gödel-number of $H(h)$ and so

$$d(h) \notin P \iff H(h) \notin \mathcal{P}.$$

So we have

$$H(h) \in \mathcal{T} \iff H(h) \notin \mathcal{P}.$$

If now $H(h) \in \mathcal{P}$, then $H(h) \in \mathcal{T}$. By the above equivalence, $H(h) \notin \mathcal{P}$, a contradiction. Hence $H(h) \notin \mathcal{P}$. By the above equivalence again, $H(h) \in \mathcal{T}$. This means that $H(h)$ is true but not provable in $\mathcal{L}$.   □

5.4 A Model-Theoretic Proof of the First Incompleteness Theorem from Tennenbaum's Theorem

We stated Tennenbaum's Theorem in Section 2.3.3, which says that the arithmetic operations of a nonstandard, countable model of *PA* cannot be recursive. A generalization of Tennenbaum's Theorem says that in a nonstandard model every set in the *standard system* is recursive in the plus and times of the model.[133] So if plus and times are recursive then every set in the standard system is recursive. But this contradicts the fact that with recursively inseparable sets one can show that there is always a nonrecursive set in the standard system.[134]

Now to Gödel's Incompleteness Theorems. By the Henkin Completeness Theorem there is a Δ_2^0 nonstandard model M of *PA*, that is, a nonstandard model $(\omega, +^M, \times^M)$, where both $+^M$ and $\times^M$ are Δ_2^0-predicates on the natural numbers. By Tennenbaum's Theorem, every set in the standard system of M is recursive in the plus and times of the model and hence Δ_2^0. Suppose M were an elementary extension of the standard model. Then every arithmetical set belongs to the standard system of M. Hence every arithmetical set is recursive in the plus and times of M. Hence these plus and times cannot be themselves arithmetical, by the hierarchy theorem of arithmetic sets asserting that the hierarchy is a strict one.[135]

Hence M cannot be an elementary extension of the standard model. Now let ψ be a sentence that is true in the standard model but false in M. Then ψ is independent of *PA*.

---

[133] A set of natural numbers X belongs to the standard system of a model of arithmetic $\mathfrak{M}$ if it is parametrically definable in the model, i.e., if for some a formula ϕ, $X = \{n \in \mathbb{N} | \mathfrak{M} \models \phi(\bar{n}, a_1, \ldots, a_n), a_i \in \mathfrak{M}\}$.

[134] See Smoryniski [120]. See also Kossak and Schmerl [66] and Kaye [66].

[135] This use of hierarchy theorem can be avoided, according to Smorynski, in which case we obtain another genuinely diagonal-free proof.

6 Mathematical Incompleteness

We begin not with Gödel but with Tarski. Tarski's conceptualization of "the mathematical," as he called it, a conceptualization that grew out of a mixture of influences ranging from the algebraic school associated with Peirce and Schröder in the nineteenth century, to the sometime antifoundationalism of the Warsaw School and to the analysis of geometric notions pursued by contemporary Polish mathematicians,[136] would contribute – if not found – a stream of research in model theory that prioritizes the *suppression* of syntax and logic in one form or another, and the *forefronting* of semantic concepts.

Tarski instrumentalized the "the mathematical" in the form of a concrete program: convert metamathematical theorems into "mathematical" ones. Tarski's 1929 theorem characterizing the sets definable in the first-order theory of real closed fields is a prime example; a set of real numbers is definable in that theory if it is a finite union of intervals of the real line.[137] What did "the mathematical" mean, exactly, for Tarski? Judging from the theorems, this refers to the elimination of metamathematical concepts from statements and proofs of, for example, the Löwenheim-Skolem Theorem, or the Completeness Theorem, by reformulating metamathematical concepts (such as elementary equivalence) in natural language, with no mention of syntax or semantics – never mind that a distinction might be drawn between the two.

Here is Vaught in 1986 [133], commenting on Tarski's 1950 ICM Lecture:

> An additional feature is that in the whole presentation Tarski (returning to and expanding his old methods from [123]) manages to define notions like "EC class" without any mention of a formalized language. Tarski liked the idea of replacing a "metamathematical" definition by a "mathematical" one; and was even more pleased by a "very mathematical" one such as Birkhoff's definition [6] of equational class. Later on he very much liked the "purely mathematical" definition of $\mathfrak{A} \equiv \mathfrak{B}$ by R.Fraïssé [elementary equivalence in terms of EF games; [29]], and still later the definition using ultraproducts (see below) [of Keisler/Shelah; [67], [115]]. These very suggestive intuitive ideas may be without a precise content, as a precise distinction between "mathematical" and "metamathematical" might well be considered to be impossible because of Tarski's definition of truth! Of course it is only in proofs that mathematicians must be precise. In the important matter of selecting what to think about, anything goes![138]

---

[136] See, for example, [25].

[137] See [72] for an extended analysis of this move of Tarski's.

[138] [133], p. 875. Errata in [132]. Birkhoff's theorem characterizes an equational class by means of set-theoretical closure operations, together with the notion of homomorphism. Precisely, a class of structures is an equational class if and only if it is closed under subalgebra, direct

Vaught's qualms with defining "the mathematical" aside, the point here is that this mathematical orientation of Tarski's would be adopted by the logical community, not necessarily with regard to metamathematical concepts in general but with regard to the Incompleteness Theorems, in the form: find *mathematical* formulations of those theorems. And while this was very likely done without any reference to Tarski, nevertheless a similar set of pressures were likely in play.

As we noted, Gödel already observed that his undecidable sentence can be made arithmetical, involving a string of alternating quantifiers followed by a Diophantine equation. By the celebrated MRDP Theorem,[139] we know that this string of quantifiers can be made existential. This led to the existence of *universal* Diophantine polynomials.[140] Of course, Diophantine problems are certainly mathematical! It must be said, though, that those arising from the Incompleteness Theorems are still based essentially on coding.

Coding aside, there is a powerful moral here: the MRDP Theorem together with, for example, the Second Incompleteness Theorem generates a host of independent Diophantine statements. For example, consider the standard consistency statement for *ZFC*, that is, $\forall x \neg B(x, \overline{\ulcorner 0 = 1 \urcorner})$ (taking $B(x,y)$ to mean as usual "x is a proof of the formula with Gödel number y." By the MRDP Theorem this is equivalent to a Diophantine equation (with natural number coefficients!)) prefixed by a universal quantifier. By the Second Incompleteness Theorem the question whether this equation has integer solutions is independent of *ZFC*.

Will these Diophantine equations cause trouble for the number theorist? In the opening of this Element we referred to the idea of a *cordon sanitaire* walling classical mathematics off from incompleteness. Macintyre's rather peckish [92] is optimistic that the walls will hold:

> The number theorists are keenly aware of issues of effectivity . . . and indeed, of relative effectivity. Moreover, each of the classical finiteness theorems is currently lacking expected effective information. However, there is not the slightest shred of evidence of some deep-rooted ineffectivity.[141]

In an interesting suggestion in the paper Macintyre identifies "the problem":

---

product, and homomorphic images. As for the EF or Ehrenfeucht-Fraïssé games, the idea here is of a logic being given by a game.

[139] See Section 2.4.2.

[140] A Diophantine polynomial P is said to be universal if for every r.e. set A and for all n, there is m such that $n \in A \leftrightarrow \exists x_1, \ldots \exists x_k P(x_1, \ldots, x_k, m, n) = 0$. [65] gave explicit examples and pointed out they can be of degree 4; [54] showed that a universal Diophantine polynomial cannot be of degree ≤ 2; for polynomials of degree 3 the question seems to be open.

[141] [92], p. 14.

In central parts of mathematics, one does not go looking for monsters, and one does not encourage them to intrude. One of the most deplorable effects of Gödel's work is the fixation with examining phenomena in utmost generality, in territory far beyond mathematical civilization.

Grothendieck has stressed that the foundational efforts of the analysts and general topologists create structures that are irrelevant or distracting for geometry, and indeed the impact of Gödel's incompleteness theorems on mathematics for mathematics in the tradition of Riemann or Poincaré, where algebraic topology gives the perspective. We now know (and on this, logicians and geometers interact) that there are extensive non-Gödelian (un-Gödelian?) territories in mathematics, where the category of definable sets is rich enough to support most of the constructions of algebraic and differential topology but moderate enough that Gödelian pathologies are avoided ... Of course, one has to go deeply into specifics to get these universes, whereas Gödel's theory is all purpose in most of its applications.[142]

The impulse to generalize in mathematics is very powerful – see, for example, the notion of "function" due to Leibniz. But generalization can go too far, and Macintyre's admonition to the logician is a good one – "Back to rough ground!" as Wittgenstein admonished the philosophers. That is, mathematics flourishes when it sticks to the case at hand.

Macintyre predicts that there will be no serious incursion of incompleteness into classical or, as it is sometimes called, "core" mathematics. And while he may be entirely right in his prediction how mathematics will turn out in the future, history has shown that mathematics is anything but predictable:

> The problem of deciding whether curves over $\mathbb{Q}$ have integer points is not yet known to be decidable, but there is a bodyguard of theory, quite independent of logical considerations and by now heavily supported by numerical evidence, that implies that undecidability is not to be expected. Indeed, it is to be dreaded (and this is Shafarevich's "gloomy joke") because of its implications for high theory.[143]

In any case, one cannot help but notice an interesting irony. We recounted the complex evolution of Gödel's concerns about the generality of the Incompleteness Theorems – but now Gödel's work is thought to be *too general*.

---

[142] [92], p. 14. This section is entitled "Topologie Modérée," i.e., to tame or "moderate" topology, incorporating the idea of restricting to the cases at hand. As described in [2], this means the following: "In particular, motivated by surface topology and moduli spaces of Riemann surfaces, Grothendieck calls there for a recasting of topology, in order to make it fit to the objects of semi-algebraic and semianalytic geometry, and in particular to the study of the Mumford-Deligne compactifications of moduli spaces."

[143] [92], p. 7.

6.1 Paris-Harrington

By now there are many mathematical independence results, but very likely the first of these is due to Paris and Harrington [106].[144] A strengthening of a finite Ramsey Theorem, it is an easy consequence of the infinite Ramsey Theorem and therefore provable in *ZF*. However, it is unprovable in *PA*, and indeed independent of *PA*. Why? If this Ramsey Theorem is added to *PA*, one can prove *Con(PA)*. Since *Con(PA)* is unprovable in *PA*, so is this Ramsey Theorem. An interesting feature of the proof is that if $f(n)$ denotes the minimum size of a finite set where we can get a so-called relatively large homogeneous set of size n, then f grows faster than any function that is provably recursive in *PA*. This led to the investigation of so-called rapidly growing Ramsey functions, all related to independent statements for *PA* and its extensions.[145]

Ramsey's Theorem[146] says that if I is an infinite set, n, m are natural numbers, and the subsets of I of size n are divided into m colors, then there is an infinite subset H of I such that all subsets of H of size n are in the same class. This is denoted symbolically as

$$\forall n \forall m (\aleph_0 \to (\aleph_0)^n_m). \tag{6.1}$$

If we think of the division into m classes as a *coloring* of the subsets by m colors, then H is *homogeneous* in the sense that all subsets of size n have the same color. Instead of an infinite set I we can also do the same for finite sets. This is Finite Ramsey's Theorem, which states that if n, m, k are natural numbers and the subsets of size n of a sufficiently large finite set $1, \ldots, r$ are divided into m classes, then there is a subset H of $1, \ldots, r$ of size k, all subsets of size n of which are in the same class. In other words, if the subsets of size n of a sufficiently large finite set $1, \ldots, r$ are colored with m color then there is a homogeneous subset H of $1, \ldots, r$ of size k. This is written symbolically as

$$\forall n \forall m \forall k \exists r (r \to (k)^n_m). \tag{6.2}$$

Naturally, when n, m, k are given, the smallest r for which this is true may be quite large, typically exponentially larger than n, m, k. Nevertheless Finite Ramsey's Theorem is provable in *PA*.

We can modify the coloring condition of Finite Ramsey's Theorem as follows. We say that *H is relatively large* if H is as large as the number that is the minimum number of H. With this modification Finite Ramsey's Theorem

---

[144] For a revisionist history see [83].

[145] See [73].

[146] See, e.g., [51].

now becomes: if the subsets of size n of a sufficiently large finite set $1, \ldots, r$ are colored with m colors, then there is a *relatively large* homogeneous subset H of $1, \ldots, r$ of size k. This is written symbolically as

$$\forall n \forall m \forall k \exists r (r \underset{*}{\rightarrow} (k)_m^n). \tag{6.3}$$

Now with this slight modification, (6.3) becomes suddenly unprovable in *PA*! It is provable in set theory (by means of the infinite Ramsey's Theorem), so it is actually independent of *PA*, assuming (a bit more than) the consistency of *PA*.

The Paris-Harrington statement appears to be a purely mathematical example of the incompleteness of *PA* – mathematical in Tarski's sense, that is – because of its resemblance to (6.3) to (6.2), and because of the absence of metamathematical concepts. As many have pointed out, however, the concept of "relatively large" is self-referential in flavor, as it is required that the size of the homogeneous set is at least the minimum of the very same set. However, the self-reference appears to be very slight. On the other hand, (6.3) is equivalent in *PA* to 1-consistency, that is, to the Σ_1-Reflection Principle that any provable Σ_1-sentence is true, which is provable in stronger theories like ATR_0 and ZFC. So (6.3) apparently has some metamathematical content.

6.2 Kruskal's Theorem

Kruskal's Theorem is the following. Let $\{T_k\}$, $k \in \mathbb{N}$ be an infinite sequence of finite trees. Then there exist indices $i, j \in \mathbb{N}$ with $i < j$ such that T_i is inf-preservingly-embeddable into T_j, that is, there exists a one-to-one, inf- and order-preserving mapping of T_i into T_j.

Friedman's program (see below) emphasizes finding finitary independence, but Kruskal's Theorem is not considered to be finitary, referring as it does to infinite sequences. By compactness, a finitary corollary of the theorem can be proved. Suppose m is given. There is n such that if $T_0, T_1, \ldots, T_n$ is a sequence of finite trees in which every tree T_k has at most $m + k$ vertices. Then there are $i < j$ such that T_i can be inf-preservingly embedded in T_j. Friedman [35] proved that the finitary statement implies the 1-consistency of ATR_0,[147] and therefore by Gödel's Second Incompleteness Theorem the statement cannot be proved in ATR_0.[148]

---

[147] ATR_0 is the formal system of arithmetical transfinite recursion with quantifier-free induction on the natural numbers.

[148] See Simpson's [119] for this and other related results. See also [4] for further discussion.

6.3 Weiermann's Phase Transition Results

A fascinating development in this area involves the phase transition results (so-called) due to Andreas Weiermann [137] dating from 2009. Weiermann describes phase transitions as follows:

> Phase transition is a type of behaviour wherein small changes of a parameter of a system cause dramatic shifts in some globally observed behaviour of the system, such shifts being usually marked by a sharp 'threshold point'. (Everyday life examples of such thresholds are ice melting and water boiling temperatures.) This kind of phenomenon nowadays occurs throughout many mathematical and computational disciplines...[149]

As it turns out, phase transitions turn up in the Incompleteness Theorems, in the sense that if one parametrizes certain versions of them, for example, in the form of Friedman's miniaturization of Kruskal's Theorem, then explicit values of the parameters can be calculated, so that below the value the statement is provable, and above the value the statement becomes unprovable. As Weiermann explains:

> [t]he underlying idea is roughly speaking as follows. Let us assume that A is a given assertion in the language of first order Peano arithmetic (PA) which is parametrized with a non-negative rational number r and that $A(r)$ is true for all values of r. Let us further assume that $A(r)$ is unprovable for large enough values of r and that this property is monotone in the following sense: if $r < s$ and $A(r)$ does not follow from PA then $A(s)$ also does not follow from PA. Moreover assume that for small enough values of r the assertion $A(r)$ does follow from PA. In this situation there will be a phase transition threshold ρ ...given by the resulting Dedekind cut. Determining ρ will in general provide valuable information about the general question: What makes a true assertion A unprovable from PA?
>
> For Kruskal's theorem the critical value for ρ is given by $ln(2)/ln(\alpha)$, (where α, the so called Otter's tree constant, has numerical value $2.95576\ldots$). (It is currently not known whether it is rational or algebraic....)

These phase transition results are profound and deeply interesting, but they have not drawn the philosophical attention they deserve.

7 Set Theoretical Incompleteness

The logician's search for natural independence, that is, for statements independent of a given theory that do not involve diagonalization or self-reference,

---

[149] [137], p. 241. In the author's [72] the phenomenon of phases transition is referred to as "entanglement," which occurs when small changes in syntax, or in the formalism more broadly, induce global changes. For example, the so-called 0–1 laws due to Fagin are sensitive to signature in the sense that they hold for relational languages, but fail if the language contains function symbols.

and that are mathematical in flavor, is amply rewarded in set theory. That is, in addition to Gödel sentences involving consistency or asserting unprovability of the Gödel sentence, a fairly large number of natural, set-theoretical independent statements have been found. One such has been discussed already in Section 5.1, namely the Second Incompleteness Theorem in the form of the unprovability of the existence of inaccessible cardinals. But others were soon to follow, particularly after the invention of forcing in 1963.

Before turning to the most prominent of these, namely the continuum hypothesis (CH), note that the existence statement for any so-called large cardinal, from Mahlo and weakly compact up to supercompact and beyond, will be independent of *ZFC*, as these are all inaccessible. So here is a plethora of naturally occurring independent set-theoretical statements. As for the CH, due to Cantor and first on Hilbert's famous list of open problems given at the Paris ICM in 1900, it states that an infinite set of real numbers must either be countable, or of the same size as the entire set of real numbers. Gödel showed in 1937 [41] that the CH cannot be disproved from the axioms of *ZFC*, that is, *ZFC* + CH is consistent. Cohen proved the consistency of *ZFC* + not-CH in 1963, for which he won a Fields Medal.

Is the CH important for mathematics? As it turns out, mathematicians seem to do very well in spite of not knowing the size of the continuum – the size, that is, as measured by the $\aleph$-hierarchy, as of course it can easily be shown that the continuum is of size $2^{\aleph_0}$. In a situation analogous to the case of mathematical incompleteness relative to Peano Arithmetic, set theorists began to search for independence results of a more concrete nature – statements that are entirely mathematical, in Tarski's sense of mathematical, but not involving, for example, cardinality. The following is a sample of some of these.

Borel's conjecture that strong measure zero sets are countable. A subset A of the real line is said to be of *strong measure zero* if for every sequence α_n of positive reals there exists a sequence I_n, $n \in \mathbb{N}$ of intervals such that $|I_n| < \alpha_n$ for all n and $A \subseteq \bigcup I_n$. Borel conjectured that every strong measure zero set is countable. As it turns out this is independent of *ZFC*, as proved by Sierpinski [118], for the consistency of the negation, and Laver [87] for the consistency.

Borel Determinacy and Zermelo Set Theory. Consider the following two-player game. A subset A of the unit interval is named at the outset. Players then take turns choosing x_i and $y_i \in \{0,1\}$. Player I wins if the sequence $\langle x_0, y_0, x_1, y_1 \ldots \rangle$, interpreted as an element of the unit interval, is in A. Player II wins if the sequence is not in A. We say that the set A is *determined* if this game is determined, meaning that one of the players has a winning strategy. The Axiom of Determinacy (AD) states that every set of reals is determined.

AD is incompatible with the Axiom of Choice but holds in $L(R)$,[150] assuming large cardinals. Closed sets are determined and Borel sets are determined, a result due to Martin [96].[151] Friedman [32] proved that Borel Determinacy is unprovable in Zermelo's set theory,[152] in that the proof is impossible without $\aleph_\alpha$ iterations of the power set axiom for all $\alpha < \omega_1$.

Friedman's concrete independence. Friedman's longstanding *concrete independence program* seeks mathematical statements that are independent of *ZFC*. We mentioned the finitary version of Kruskal's Theorem that Friedman proved to be independent; here the focus is on the existence of large cardinals.

A typical result among many of this kind due to Friedman in this brilliant line of research is the following [36]. The statement "There is a set E such that every transitive set not in E has a four element $\subset$-chain" is equivalent over *ZFC* to the existence of a subtle cardinal. Hence it cannot be proved from *ZFC* but it is true if we assume a subtle cardinal. Subtle cardinals are strongly inaccessible and in size roughly between weakly compact and measurable.[153]

Projective determinacy and regularity properties of the reals. The classical descriptive set theory project of the 1920s and 1930s, which sought to classify point classes of the descriptive hierarchy, so-called, came to a halt in the 1930s over the problem of extending the so-called regularity properties to the projective sets.[154] As Luzin famously said:

> [o]ne does not know and *one will never know* of the family of projective sets, although it has cardinality $2^{\aleph_0}$ and consists of effective sets, whether every member has cardinality $2^{\aleph_0}$ if it is uncountable, has the Baire property, or is even Lebesgue measurable.[155]

In an astonishing achievement due to Martin and Steel [97] and Woodin [140] the problem was finally solved; projective sets are determined, assuming large

---

[150] $L(R)$ is the smallest transitive inner model of *ZF* containing all the ordinals and all the reals.

[151] An earlier proof of Borel Determinacy also due to Martin used a measurable cardinal [95]. This is an example of large cardinals having verifiable consequences, in Gödel's sense of the phrase here, i.e., it was subsequently proved without using measurables, and the measurables in turn were verified by their having led to the "correct" result.

[152] Zermelo's set theory lacks the Replacement Axiom.

[153] For other results in this vein see Friedman's [34]. See also www.math.ohio-state.edu/~friedman/manuscripts.html, which is an invaluable source of theorems and conjectures in this line of research (especially 49–51), and also in Friedman's more recent program of tangible incompleteness.

[154] The regularity properties are just those already mentioned, which hold for the Borel sets: Lebesgue measurability, Baire property, and the perfect set property. The projective sets are obtained from closed sets by iterating taking complements and continuous images. The principle known as projective determinacy (PD) is independent.

[155] See [91].

cardinals. This implies many regularity properties for projective sets of reals (see, e.g., [100]).

Whitehead's Conjecture. In 1974 Shelah [116] surprised algebraists by proving that a problem about uncountable abelian groups attributed to Whitehead (namely whether every Z-module satisfying $\text{Ext}(A, Z) = 0$ is free) was undecidable in ZFC. He later showed – in one of his first ventures in using forcing – that the problem cannot be decided even assuming GCH. This and much subsequent work by him in this area has had a large impact.

8 Further Philosophical Consequences of the Incompleteness Theorems

We have treated the philosophical consequences of the Incompleteness Theorems throughout this book, as they arise. Here we take up some further issues.

The consequences of the Incompleteness Theorems for the Hilbert Program center mainly around the question whether the Second Incompleteness Theorem undermines the plank of that program having to do with the demand for an internal *finitary* consistency proof as we saw.[156] The consensus seems to be in favor, but there are a number of important objections having to do with the intensional adequacy of the provability predicate of the theory in question (as we also noted). As for the demand for completeness, in the sense that every mathematical proposition formulated in an appropriate system is provable or refutable, this desideratum of the Hilbert Program would seem to be straightforwardly impossible to satisfy.

It is all the more striking, then, that Gödel, after some wavering throughout the 1930s and 1940s on the question whether there were absolutely undecidable propositions,[157] would adopt this position: "As to problems with the answer Yes or No, the conviction that they are always decidable remains untouched by these results [i.e., the Incompleteness Theorems]."

8.1 Absolute Undecidability

The above remark was made in the 1930s while Gödel still entertained the proposition that there are *absolutely undecidable* statements, using the Continuum Hypothesis (CH) as an example (see below). This is in contrast to statements

---

[156] This depends on how one interprets the Hilbert Program, as of course the First Incompleteness Theorem also can be interpreted as undermining that Program. See Zach's writings on the Hilbert Program, among which is [141]. See also Raatikainen's [110].

[157] See Gödel's Brown Lecture *193?* in [45]. Some papers on absolute undecidability include [131], Koellner's [78], and Davis's [13].

arising from "residual" or "formal incompleteness," that is, artifacts of formalization in the form of the First and Second Incompleteness Theorems, which are solvable if we pass to higher systems as we saw in Section 2.4.1, which treated Gödel's mysterious footnote 48a.

As for what one might think of as a deeper form of incompleteness, involving independent set-theoretic statements, this is a different matter entirely.[158] We saw in Section 6 above some examples of set-theoretic and also quite mathematical statements that are independent of the *ZFC* axioms, where the independence is not obtained via the Incompleteness Theorems but by other means, for example, the forcing method. The question whether such independence is a permanent feature of set-theoretic practice is much debated in the philosophy of set theory today. Some have argued that the concept of set is inherently vague, so that statements such as the CH are underdetermined by the concept of set;[159] others, being very much inspired by Gödel's remarks starting in the 1940s, have argued that set-theoretic independence is impermanent, that a natural extension of the *ZFC* will eventually emerge, which will decide the set-theoretic questions of interest. Koellner [78] advocates the latter position:

> Starting with a generally non-skeptical stance toward set theory I will argue that there is a remarkable amount of structure and unity beyond *ZFC* and that a network of results in modern set theory make for a compelling case for new axioms that settle many questions undecided by *ZFC*. I will argue that most of the candidates proposed as instances of absolute undecidability have been settled and that there is not currently a good argument to the effect that a given sentence is absolutely undecidable.

The evolution of Gödel's own position regarding the decidability of such statements begins with Gödel advocating for the absolute *un*decidability of statements like the CH in the early 1930s.[160] But then, as Karl Menger recalls in [131], Gödel began to believe in around 1933 that "the right (*die rechten*, sometimes he said *die richtigen*) axioms of set theory had not yet been found."

---

[158] The authors of [131] refer to this as "conceptual incompleteness."

[159] See, e.g., Feferman's "Is the Continuum Hypothesis a definite mathematical problem?" http://math.stanford.edu/~feferman/papers/IsCHdefinite.pdf.

[160] For example in his Brown Lecture he remarks:

> However, I would not leave it unmentioned that apparently there do exist questions of a very similar structure which very likely are really undecidable in the sense which I explained first. The difference in the structure of these problems is only that also variables for real numbers appear in this polynomial. Questions connected with Cantor's continuum hypothesis lead to problems of this type. So far I have not been able to prove their undecidability, but there are considerations which make it highly plausible that they really are undecidable.

1931?, [45], p. 35.

By 1946–1947 this conviction ripened into a full program, grounded in the idea of conceptual analysis of the meaning of the concept of set and of the related, self-evident, and *true* axioms, and directed toward eliminating set-theoretic independence of this kind:

> This scarcity of results, even as to the most fundamental questions in this field, may be due to some extent to purely mathematical difficulties; it seems, however ...that there are also deeper reasons behind it and that a complete solution of these problems can be obtained only by a more profound analysis (than mathematics is accustomed to give) of the meanings of the terms occurring in them (such as "set," "one-to-one correspondence," etc.) and of the axioms underlying their use.[161]

"Gödel's Program," as it is now known, would occupy Gödel's attention for most of the rest of his life. What he advocated in the direction of eliminating set-theoretic independence would inspire future generations of set theorists and philosophers to follow him in deepening and sharpening the program, so that now the literature on the justification of new axioms for set theory alone is by now philosophically significant and quite substantial. Landmark texts in the area include [26], due to Feferman, Friedman, Maddy and Steel; Maddy's work on justification including [93] and other works, which are written from a naturalistic point of view; and Woodin's [139], among his many other works advocating specific new axioms. An interesting new proposal for the decidability of the CH involving the model-theoretic concepts of model companion and model completeness is explained in Viale's "The model-companionship spectrum of set theory, generic absoluteness, and the Continuum problem."[162]

Gödel's Program for large cardinals grew out of his contemplation of the concept of absolute undecidability, but his treatment of absolute undecidability also gave rise to a separate chain of ideas involving the computational nature of the mind. In his 1951 Gibbs Lecture, Gödel defines absolute undecidability to mean "undecidable, not just within some particular axiomatic system, but by any mathematical proof the human mind can conceive."[163] Considering the possibility of absolutely undecidable Π_2 Diophantine sentences, he then goes on to state what became known as his "disjunctive theorem":

> Either mathematics is incompletable in this sense, that its evident axioms can never be comprised in a finite rule, that is to say, the human mind (even within the realm of pure mathematics) infinitely surpasses the powers of any finite machine, or else there exist absolutely unsolvable Diophantine problems of

---

[161] [43], p. 179. For a detailed analysis of Gödel's evolving views on absolute undecidability see [131].

[162] See also Viale and Venturi's [134].

[163] [45], p. 103.

the type specified (where the case that both terms of the disjunction are true is not excluded, so that there are, strictly speaking, three alternatives).

Note that, as Parsons has pointed out,[164] the second alternative is not incompatible with Gödel's well-known realist stance, that "mathematics describes a non-sensual reality, which exists independently both of the acts and [of] the dispositions of the human mind and is only perceived, and probably perceived very incompletely, by the human mind."[165] But Gödel mainly argued for the *first* alternative, and on numerous occasions, including in a *Time* magazine publication in which he wanted it reported that "Either mathematics is too big for the human mind,' he says, 'or the human mind is more than a machine.' He hopes to prove the latter."[166]

The question whether "the mind is a Turing machine," or more precisely the question whether the Incompleteness Theorems challenge the idea that strictly computational models of the mind/consciousness can be given, has generated a large literature, mainly stimulated by Penrose's argument in his *Shadows of the mind: a search for the missing science of consciousness* [109], together with the earlier arguments of Lucas [90]. Most philosophers, including Feferman [23] and Burgess [7], have rejected Penrose's arguments – though, as Burgess says, "logicians are not unanimously agreed as to where precisely the fallacy in their argument lies." Limitations of space preclude any further treatment of the Lucas–Penrose debate in these pages.[167]

8.2 Intuition, Insight, and Meaning

Incompleteness infects every formalism of interest, in that every attempt to concretize our mathematical knowledge through formalization must inevitably fail, if we desire completeness – and yet human beings can acquire genuine mathematical knowledge. This is because human beings are equipped, according to Gödel, with the capacity to grasp genuine mathematical content. Where does this capacity come from? And does this mean that mathematical content is not formal? In his 1958 *Dialectica* paper, which is one of Gödel's philosophically richest and most beautiful essays, Gödel speaks of a bifurcated mental capacity, involving on one level intuition of concrete evidence and on a second level insight into the meanings of abstract or higher-order objects:

> Consequently, since finitary mathematics is defined as the mathematics in which evidence rests on what is *intuitive*, certain *abstract* notions are

---

[164] [107], p. 52.
[165] [45], p. 323.
[166] [5], p. 53.
[167] For a recent reference on this issue see [1].

required for the proof of the consistency of number theory ... Here, by abstract (or nonintuitive) notions we must understand those that are essentially of second or higher order, that is, notions that do not involve properties or relations of *concrete objects* (for example, of combinations of signs), but that relate to *mental constructs* (for example, proofs, meaningful statements, and so on); and in the proofs we make use of insights, into these mental constructs, that spring not from the combinatorial (spatiotemporal) properties of the sign combinations representing the proofs, but only from their *meaning*.[168]

Gödel indicates in a footnote to the above paragraph that his notion of intuition is drawn from the formulation in Hilbert's 1926 paper "On the infinite" [63], but Gödel's notion of intuition changed over time. Many have written about Gödel's notion of intuition, also in relation to Hilbert's avowedly Kantian notion, including Tait [122]. As Tait points out in that essay, "Gödel simply doesn't see the 'finite' in 'finitary': He sees 'concrete intuition' instead, and he questions Hilbert's restriction to the concrete." Tait discusses Gödel's attempt to give an explicit bound on finitism, in the form of the ordinal ϵ_0:

Early in his career, he believed that finitism (in Hilbert's sense) is open-ended, in the sense that no correct formal system can be known to formalize all finitist proofs and, in particular, all possible finitist proofs of consistency of first-order number theory, *PA*; but starting in the *Dialectica* paper, he expressed in writing the view that ϵ_0 is an upper bound on the finitist ordinals, and that, therefore, the consistency of *PA*, cannot be finitistically proved ... Incidentally, the analysis he gives of what should count as a finitist ordinal in [1958], [1972] should in fact lead to the bound ω^ω, the ordinal of primitive recursive arithmetic, *PRA*...[169]

As an aside, Gödel's attempt to give a mathematically explicit bound on finitism in the form of an ordinal is symptomatic of his general philosophical method, which can very roughly be described as philosophy in the form of theorems. Moreover, short of an exact theorem, the basic stance is explicitly speculative, a view that is related to Gödel's "rational optimism." Whether it be on the limits of intuitionism, leading to the remarkable theorem *1933e* that Heyting Arithmetic is equiconsistent with classical arithmetic, or the theorem *1932* that intuitionistic propositional logic cannot be thought of as a finitely valued logic, or indeed in 1931, in the very beginning, that truth separates from proof, philosophy, for Gödel, was to be a form of *strenge Wissenschaft*.

---

[168] [43], p. 241. Emphasis Gödel's.
[169] [122], p. 88.

Returning to Gödel's concept of concrete intuiton, Tait continues:

> Gödel seems to have had in mind a kind of evidence that one might say rests on abstract intuition, that goes beyond concrete intuition, but remains logic free. This seems to be the idea that he was trying to work out – but never succeeded – in the *Dialectica* paper and its revision (which he never released for publication). But it is a different conception of intuition from the kind of intuition he speaks of in [Gödel *1961/?*; Gödel *1964*], where intuition is invoked as a source of new axioms in set theory. Charles Parsons [108, pp. 57–58] makes the distinction between the concrete intuition of Hilbert's finitism and intuition in the sense that it is used in [Gödel *1964*; Gödel, *1961/?*] and discusses the latter in some detail. I am suggesting that for Gödel there was another conception of intuition, to which I am referring as "abstract intuition", which would play the same foundational role as concrete intuition. For the purpose of consistency proofs it was essential, on pain of circularity, that the methods used to prove consistency – finitism or proposed extensions of it – rest on a different, non-axiomatic foundation from the axiomatic theories whose consistency is to be proved.[170]

Logic and language freeness has been a running thread in this book on Gödel's Incompleteness Theorems. From Smullyan's "abstract" proof of the First Incompleteness Theorem to the subtle role of Church's Thesis in the *Entscheidungsproblem*, to, now, Gödel's concept of abstract intuition, what these all show is that to be concerned with the *formal* is to be concerned at the same time with its limits.

8.3 Conclusion

The Incompleteness Theorems cut across the formal/informal divide like a figure skater executing figure-eights on the surface of the ice. If the authors of books in this series are encouraged to express their own view of the matter at hand, here, then, are two of mine. First, what the Incompleteness Theorems demonstrate is the enduring plasticity of the syntax/semantics distinction, to wit: Gödel's *1931* gives us the First Incompleteness Theorem in fully syntactic form – and yet one can view that theorem in a myriad of different ways *semantically*. There is also the blurring of the syntax/semantics distinction. The theorem depends, as we saw, on the concept of strong representability, but this can serve as a device for masking semantic content, rendering formal objects as *geneological isolates*.[171] Finally, and speaking to the fragility of the distinction,

---

[170] [122], p. 94. See also Parsons's "Platonism and mathematical intuition in Kurt Gödel's thought" [107], Burgess's "Intuitions of three kinds in Gödel's views on the continuum" in [70], Tieszen's "Gödel and the intuition of concepts" [126], van Atten and Kennedy's [130], and the various essays in van Atten's [129].

[171] The phrase "geneological isolate" appears in Section 2.3.1.

there is deviance, the fact that the Incompleteness Theorems are uncommonly sensitive to disturbances in the syntax of the formalism in question.

Second, consider the axioms of Robinson arithmetic Q.[172] The theory is incomplete and, more than that, essentially incomplete:

1. $\neg s(x) = 0$
2. $s(x) = s(y) \rightarrow x = y$
3. $y = 0 \vee \exists x(s(x) = y)$
4. $x + 0 = x$
5. $x + s(y) = s(x + y)$
6. $x \cdot 0 = 0$
7. $x \cdot s(y) = x \cdot y + x$

Logicians know vastly more about the Incompleteness Theorems than they knew in 1931. So it is easy to lose one's sense of wonder at the fact that such a *blindingly obvious* set of axioms as those above is essentially incomplete and essentially undecidable, meaning *all* axiomatizable consistent extensions are incomplete and undecidable. Hold on to that wonder! For it teaches us that when it comes to our attempt to master the conceptual order, whether it be in mathematics or for that matter in any other domain, we will always fail – and indeed in this case *more than any other* we should be glad to fail, for failure was clearly the better, the more profound, outcome.

---

[172] See Section G.3.

Glossary

G.1 Peano Arithmetic PA

The language of Peano Arithmetic PA has $=$, a constant symbol $\bar{0}$, one-place function symbol s, and two-place function symbols $+$ and $\cdot$. The axioms of PA are the usual axioms for equality and

1. $\neg s(x) = \bar{0}$
2. $s(x) = s(y) \rightarrow x = y$
3. $x + \bar{0} = x$
4. $x + s(y) = s(x + y)$
5. $x \cdot \bar{0} = \bar{0}$
6. $x \cdot s(y) = (x \cdot y) + x$
7. for each formula $\phi(x_0, \ldots, x_n)$ of the language of PA the axiom

$$(\phi(\bar{0}, x_1, \ldots, x_n) \wedge \forall x(\phi(x, x_1, \ldots, x_n) \rightarrow \phi(s(x), x_1, \ldots, x_n)))$$
$$\rightarrow \forall x \phi(x, x_1, \ldots, x_n).$$

G.2 Primitive recursive arithmetic PRA

The language of PRA has $=$, a constant symbol $\bar{0}$, variables x_n, $(n < \omega)$, one-place function symbols $\bar{Z}$ and s, k-place function symbols $\overline{P_i^k}$ for each i and k with $1 \leq i \leq k < \omega$, and additional function symbols, which are introduced as follows. If $\bar{g}$ is an m-place function symbol and $\bar{h}_1, \ldots, \bar{h}_m$ are k-place function symbols, then $\bar{f} = C(\bar{g}, \bar{h}_1, \ldots, \bar{h}_m)$ is a k-place function symbol. If $\bar{g}$ is a k-place function symbol and $\bar{h}$ is a $(k + 2)$-place function symbol, then $\bar{f} = R(\bar{g}, \bar{h})$ is a $(k + 1)$-place function symbol. The axioms of PRA are the usual axioms for equality and

1. $\bar{Z}(x) = 0$
2. $s(x) = s(y) \rightarrow x = y$
3. $x \neq \bar{0} \leftrightarrow \exists y(s(y) = x)$
4. $\overline{P_i^k}(x_1, \ldots, x_k) = x_i$
5. $\bar{f}(x_1, \ldots, x_k) = \bar{g}(\bar{h}_1(x_1, \ldots, x_k), \ldots, \bar{h}_m(x_1, \ldots, x_k))$,
   when $\bar{f} = C(\bar{g}, \bar{h}_1, \ldots, \bar{h}_m)$
6. $\bar{f}(0, x_1, \ldots, x_k) = \bar{g}(x_1, \ldots, x_k)$,
   $\bar{f}(s(y), x_1, \ldots, x_k) = \bar{h}(y, \bar{f}(y, x_1, \ldots, x_k), x_1, \ldots, x_k)$,
   whenever $\bar{f} = R(\bar{g}, \bar{h})$

7. $(\theta(\bar{0}) \wedge \forall x(\theta(x) \rightarrow \theta(s(x)))) \rightarrow \forall x \theta(x)$,

   where $\theta(x)$ is any quantifier-free formula in the language of *PRA* with a distinguished free-number variable x.

G.3 The Theory Q

The language of Q is the same as the language of *PA*. Its axioms are:

1. $\neg s(x) = 0$
2. $s(x) = s(y) \rightarrow x = y$
3. $y = 0 \vee \exists x(s(x) = y)$
4. $x + 0 = x$
5. $x + s(y) = s(x + y)$
6. $x \cdot 0 = 0$
7. $x \cdot s(y) = x \cdot y + x$

G.4 The Theory R

The language of R is the same as the language of *PA*. This theory is notable because it is weaker than Q but, then again, it is not finitely axiomatizable. The axioms are as follows, for all m and n:

R1 $\bar{n} + \bar{m} = \overline{n + m}$

R2 $\bar{n} \cdot \bar{m} = \overline{n \cdot m}$

R3 $\neg \bar{n} = \bar{m}$, for $n \neq m$

R4 $\exists y(y + x = \bar{n}) \rightarrow (x = \bar{0} \vee x = \bar{1} \vee \ldots \vee x = \bar{n})$

R5 $\exists y(y + x = \bar{n}) \vee \exists y(y + \bar{n} = x)$

G.5 The Arithmetical Hierarchy

1. The Δ_0^0-relations are the recursive relations. Another notation is Σ_0^0 or Π_0^0.
2. The Σ_{n+1}^0-relations are the relations $R(m_1, \ldots, m_n)$ that satisfy

$$R(m_1, \ldots, m_n) \leftrightarrow \exists a_1 \ldots \exists a_k S(a_1, \ldots, a_k, m_1, \ldots, m_n),$$

   where $S(a_1, \ldots, a_k, m_1, \ldots, m_n)$ is a Π_n^0-relation.
3. The Π_{n+1}^0-relations are the relations $R(m_1, \ldots, m_n)$ that satisfy

$$R(m_1, \ldots, m_n) \leftrightarrow \forall a_1 \ldots \forall a_k S(a_1, \ldots, a_k, m_1, \ldots, m_n),$$

   where $S(a_1, \ldots, a_k, m_1, \ldots, m_n)$ is a Σ_n^0-relation.
4. The Δ_n^0-relations are the Σ_n^0-relations that are also Π_n^0-relations.

There is also the closely related arithmetic hierarchy of *formulas* of the language of *PA*. The Σ_0-formulas are the formulas in which all quantifiers are bounded, that is, of the form $\forall x < y$ or of the form $\exists x < y$. The Σ_0-formulas are also called Π_0-formulas. The Σ_{n+1}-formulas are formulas of the form $\exists x \phi$, where ϕ is Π_n. Respectively, the Π_{n+1}-formulas are formulas of the form $\forall x \phi$, where ϕ is Σ_n. A set (or a relation) of natural numbers is called Σ_n if it can be defined on the structure $(\mathbb{N}, +, \cdot)$ by a Σ_n-formula. Respectively, a set (or a relation) is called Π_n if it can be defined on the structure $(\mathbb{N}, +, \cdot)$ by a Π_n-formula. The r.e. sets are exactly the Σ_1 sets. Thus recursive sets are exactly the Δ_1-sets. More generally Σ^0_{n+1}-relations are exactly the relations that can be defined by a Σ_{n+1}-formula, and respectively for Π_{n+1}- and Δ^0_n-relations.

References

[1] People, machines and Gödel (special issue, edited by R. Kossak). *Semiotic Studies*, 34(1), 2020.

[2] Norbert A'Campo, Lizhen Ji, and Athanase Papadopoulos. On Grothendieck's tame topology. In A. Papadopoulos (ed.), *Handbook of Teichmüller theory. Vol. VI*, volume 27 of *IRMA Lect. Math. Theor. Phys.*, pp. 521–533. Eur. Math. Soc., Zürich, 2016.

[3] Wilhelm Ackermann. Zum Hilbertschen Aufbau der reellen Zahlen. *Math. Ann.*, 99(1):118–133, 1928.

[4] Lev D. Beklemishev. Gödel's incompleteness theorems and the limits of their applicability. I. *Uspekhi Mat. Nauk*, 65(5(395)):61–106, 2010.

[5] David Bergamini. *Mathematics*. Time, New York, 1963.

[6] Garrett Birkhoff. On the structure of abstract algebras. *Math. Proc. Camb. Philos. Soc.*, 31(7):434–454, 1935.

[7] John P. Burgess. On the outside looking in: a caution about conservativeness. In S. Feferman, C. Parsons, and S. G. Simpson (eds.), *Kurt Gödel: essays for his centennial*, vol. 33 of *Lect. Notes Log.*, pp. 128–141. Association of Symbolic Logic, La Jolla, CA, 2010.

[8] Georg Cantor. Über eine Eigenschaft des Inbegriffs aller reellen algebraischen Zahlen. *J. Reine Angew. Math.*, 77:258–263, 1873.

[9] Rudolf Carnap. *Der logische Aufbau der Welt*, vol. 514 of *Philosophische Bibliothek [Philosophical Library]*. Felix Meiner Verlag, Hamburg, 1998. Reprint of the 1928 original and of the author's preface to the 1961 edition.

[10] Alonzo Church. A note on the Entscheidungsproblem. *J. Symb. Log.*, 1:40–41 (Correction 1:101–102), 1936.

[11] Martin Davis. On the theory of recursive unsolvability. Ph.D. thesis, Princeton University, 1950.

[12] Martin Davis, ed. *The undecidable*. Dover Publications Inc., Mineola, NY, 2004. Basic papers on undecidable propositions, unsolvable problems and computable functions. Corrected reprint of the 1965 original.

[13] Martin Davis. What did Gödel believe and when did he believe it? *Bull. Symb. Log.*, 11(2):194–206, 2005.

[14] Martin Davis. The incompleteness theorem. *Notices Amer. Math. Soc.*, 53(4):414–418, 2006.

[15] Martin Davis and Hilary Putnam. A computing procedure for quantification theory. *J. Assoc. Comput. Mach.*, 7:201–215, 1960.

[16] Martin Davis, Hilary Putnam, and Julia Robinson. The decision problem for exponential diophantine equations. *Ann. of Math. (2)*, 74:425–436, 1961.

[17] Richard Dedekind. *What are numbers and what should they be?* RIM Monographs in Mathematics. Research Institute for Mathematics, Orono, ME, 1995. Revised, edited, and translated from the German by H. Pogorzelski, W. Ryan, and W. Snyder.

[18] Michael Detlefsen. *Hilbert's Program: an essay on mathematical instrumentalism*. Springer, Boston, MA, 1986.

[19] Ali Enayat and Albert Visser. New constructions of satisfaction classes. In K. Fujimoto, J. M. Fernández, H. Galinon, and T. Achourioti (eds.), *Unifying the philosophy of truth*, vol. 36 of *Log. Epistemol. Unity Sci.*, pp. 321–335. Springer, Dordrecht, 2015.

[20] Solomon Feferman. Arithmetization of metamathematics in a general setting. *Fund. Math.*, 49:35–92, 1960/1961.

[21] Solomon Feferman. Transfinite recursive progressions of axiomatic theories. *J. Symbol. Log.*, 27:259–316, 1962.

[22] Solomon Feferman. Kurt Gödel: conviction and caution. *Philos. Natur.*, 21(2–4): 546–563, 1984.

[23] Solomon Feferman. Penrose's Gödelian argument: a review of *Shadows of the Mind*, by Roger Penrose. *Psyche*, 2(7):21–32, 1995.

[24] Solomon Feferman. *In the light of logic*. Logic and Computation in Philosophy. Oxford University Press, New York, 1998.

[25] Solomon Feferman. Tarski's conceptual analysis of semantical notions. In Douglas Patterson, ed., *New essays on Tarski and philosophy*, pp. 72–93. Oxford University Press, Oxford, 2008.

[26] Solomon Feferman, Harvey M. Friedman, Penelope Maddy, and John R. Steel. Does mathematics need new axioms? *Bull. Symb. Log.*, 6(4):401–446, 2000.

[27] Juliet Floyd and Aki Kanamori. Gödel vis-à-vis Russell: logic and set theory to philosophy. In G. Crocco and E.-M. Engelen (eds.), *Gödelian studies on the Max-Phil Notebooks*, vol 1. Forthcoming.

[28] Juliet Floyd and Hilary Putnam. A note on Wittgenstein's "notorious paragraph" about the Gödel theorem. *J. Philos.*, 97(11):624–632, 2000.

[29] Roland Fraïssé. Sur quelques classifications des relations, basées sur des isomorphismes restreints. II. Application aux relations d'ordre, et construction d'exemples montrant que ces classifications sont distinctes. *Publ. Sci. Univ. Alger. Sér. A.*, 2:273–295, 1954.

[30] Curtis Franks. *The autonomy of mathematical knowledge: Hilbert's program revisited.* Cambridge University Press, Cambridge, 2009.

[31] Torkel Franzén. *Inexhaustibility: a non-exhaustive treatment.*, vol. 16 of *Lect. Notes Log.*, Association for Symbolic Logic, Urbana, IL; A K Peters, Ltd., Wellesley, MA, 2004.

[32] Harvey M. Friedman. Higher set theory and mathematical practice. *Ann. Math. Logic*, 2(3):325–357, 1970/1971.

[33] Harvey M. Friedman. On the necessary use of abstract set theory. *Advances in Mathematics*, 41:209–280, 1981.

[34] Harvey M. Friedman. Finite functions and the necessary use of large cardinals. *Ann. of Math. (2)*, 148(3):803–893, 1998.

[35] Harvey M. Friedman. Internal finite tree embeddings. In W. Sieg, R. Sommer, and C. Talcott (eds.), *Reflections on the foundations of mathematics*, vol. 15 of *Lect. Notes Log.*, pp. 60–91. Association for Symbolic Logic, Urbana, IL; A K Peters, Ltd., Wellesley, MA,

[36] Harvey M. Friedman. Primitive independence results. *J. Math. Log.*, 3(1):67–83, 2003.

[37] Haim Gaifman. Naming and diagonalization, from Cantor to Gödel to Kleene. *Log. J. IGPL*, 14(5):709–728, 2006.

[38] Robin Gandy. The confluence of ideas in 1936. In R. Herken (ed.), *The universal Turing machine: a half-century survey*, pp. 55–111. Oxford University Press, New York, 1988.

[39] Gerhard Gentzen. Die Widerspruchsfreiheit der reinen Zahlentheorie. *Math. Ann.*, 112:493–565, 1936.

[40] Kurt Gödel. Über formal unentscheidbare Sätze der Principia Mathematica und verwandter Systeme I. *Monatsh. Math. Phys.*, 38(1):173–198, 1931.

[41] Kurt Gödel. The consistency of the axiom of choice and of the generalized continuum hypothesis. *Proc. Natl. Acad. Sci. USA*, 24:556–557, 1938.

[42] Kurt Gödel. *Collected works. Vol. I: Publications 1929–1936.* The Clarendon Press, Oxford University Press, New York, 1986. Edited and with a preface by S. Feferman.

[43] Kurt Gödel. *Collected works. Vol. II: Publications 1938–1974.* The Clarendon Press, Oxford University Press, New York, 1990. Edited and with a preface by S. Feferman.

[44] Kurt Gödel. *Remarks before the Princeton bicentennial conference of problems in mathematics, 1946.* In *Collected works. Vol. II: Publications 1938–1974.* The Clarendon Press, Oxford University Press, New York, 1990. Edited and with a preface by S. Feferman.

[45] Kurt Gödel. *Collected works. Vol. III: Unpublished essays and lectures.* The Clarendon Press, Oxford University Press, New York, 1995. With a preface by S. Feferman. Edited by S. Feferman, J. W. Dawson, Jr., W. Goldfarb, C. Parsons, and R. M. Solovay.

[46] Kurt Gödel. *Collected works. Vol. IV: Correspondence A–G.* The Clarendon Press, Oxford University Press, Oxford, 2003. Edited by S. Feferman, J. W. Dawson, Jr., W. Goldfarb, C. Parsons, and W. Sieg.

[47] Kurt Gödel. *Collected works. Vol. V: Correspondence H–Z.* The Clarendon Press, Oxford University Press, Oxford, 2003. Edited by S. Feferman, J. W. Dawson, Jr., W. Goldfarb, C. Parsons, and W. Sieg.

[48] Warren D. Goldfarb. The Gödel class with identity is unsolvable. *Bull. Amer. Math. Soc. (N.S.)*, 10(1):113–115, 1984.

[49] Balthasar Grabmayr. On the invariance of Gödel's second theorem with regard to numberings. *Rev. Symb. Log.*, 14(1):51–84, 2021.

[50] Balthasar Grabmayr and Albert Visser. Self-reference upfront: a study of self-referential gödel numberings. *Rev. Symb. Log.*, pp. 1–41, 2021. doi:10.1017/S1755020321000393.

[51] Ronald L. Graham, Bruce L. Rothschild, and Joel H. Spencer. *Ramsey theory.* Wiley-Interscience Series in Discrete Mathematics. John Wiley & Sons, Inc., New York, 1980.

[52] Ivor Grattan-Guinness. In memoriam Kurt Gödel: his 1931 correspondence with Zermelo on his incompletability theorem. *Historia Math.*, 6(3):294–304, 1979.

[53] Robert Gray. Georg Cantor and transcendental numbers. *Amer. Math. Monthly*, 101(9):819–832, 1994.

[54] Fritz Grunewald and Dan Segal. On the integer solutions of quadratic equations. *J. Reine Angew. Math.*, 569:13–45, 2004.

[55] Petr Hájek and Pavel Pudlák. *Metamathematics of first-order arithmetic.* Perspectives in Mathematical Logic. Springer-Verlag, Berlin, 1998. Second printing.

[56] Volker Halbach and Leon Horsten. Computational structuralism. *Philos. Math. (3)*, 13(2):174–186, 2005.

[57] Volker Halbach and Albert Visser. Self-reference in arithmetic I. *Rev. Symb. Log.*, 7(4):671–691, 2014.

[58] Volker Halbach and Albert Visser. Self-reference in arithmetic II. *Rev. Symb. Log.*, 7(4):692–712, 2014.

[59] Jacques Herbrand. *Logical writings: a translation of the ıt Écrits logiques*, Harvard University Press, Cambridge, MA, 1971. Edited by J.van Heijenoort and including contributions by C.Chevalley and A. Lautman.

[60] David Hilbert and Wilhelm Ackermann. *Grundzüge der theoretischen Logik.* Die Grundlehren der mathematischen Wissenschaften Bd. 27). VIII, 120 S.J. Springer, Berlin. 1928.

[61] David Hilbert and Paul Bernays. *Grundlagen der Mathematik. I,* 2nd edn. Die Grundlehren der mathematischen Wissenschaften, vol. 40. Springer-Verlag, Berlin, New York, 1968.

[62] David Hilbert and Paul Bernays. *Grundlagen der Mathematik. II,* 2nd edn. Zweite Auflage. Die Grundlehren der mathematischen Wissenschaften, vol. 50. Springer-Verlag, Berlin, New York, 1970.

[63] David Hilbert. On the infinite. In J. van Heijenoort (ed.), *From Frege to Gödel: A Source Book in Mathematical Logic,* pp. 367–392. Harvard University Press, Cambridge, MA, 1965.

[64] David Hilbert. *David Hilbert's lectures on the foundations of geometry, 1891–1902,* vol. 1 of *David Hilbert's Lectures on the Foundations of Mathematics and Physics 1891–1933.* Springer-Verlag, Berlin, 2004. Edited by Michael Hallett and Ulrich Majer.

[65] James P. Jones. Three universal representations of recursively enumerable sets. *J. Symb. Log.,* 43(2):335–351, 1978.

[66] Richard Kaye. *Models of Peano arithmetic,* vol. 15 of *Oxford Logic Guides.* The Clarendon Press, Oxford University Press, New York, 1991. Oxford Science Publications.

[67] H. Jerome Keisler. Ultraproducts and saturated models. *Nederl. Akad. Wetensch. Proc. Ser. A 67 = Indag. Math.,* 26:178–186, 1964.

[68] Juliette Kennedy. Turing, Gödel and the "Bright Abyss." In J. Floyd and A. Bokulich (eds), *Philosophical Explorations of the Legacy of Alan Turing,* vol. 324 of *Boston Studies in Philosophy.* Springer, Cham, 2017.

[69] Juliette Kennedy. Gödel's Thesis: an appreciation. In Mathias Baaz, Christos H. Papadimitriou, Hilary W. Putnam, Dana S. Scott, and Charles L. Harper, Jr., eds., *Kurt Gödel and the Foundations of Mathematics: Horizons of Truth.* Cambridge University Press, Cambridge, 2011.

[70] Juliette Kennedy. Gödel's 1946 Princeton Bicentennial Lecture: an appreciation. In Juliette Kennedy, ed., *Interpreting Gödel.* Cambridge University Press, Cambridge, 2014.

[71] Juliette Kennedy. Kurt Gödel. In Edward N. Zalta, ed., *The Stanford Encyclopedia of Philosophy.* Metaphysics Research Lab, Stanford University, Stanford, CA, winter edn. 2018.

[72] Juliette Kennedy. *Gödel, Tarski and the lure of natural language: logical entanglement, formalism freeness.* Cambridge University Press, Cambridge, 2020.

[73] Jussi Ketonen and Robert Solovay. Rapidly growing Ramsey functions. *Ann. of Math. (2)*, 113(2):267–314, 1981.

[74] Stephen C. Kleene. General recursive functions of natural numbers. *Math. Ann.*, 112(1):727–742, 1936.

[75] Stephen C. Kleene. On notation for ordinal numbers. *J. Symb. Log.*, 3:150–155, 1938.

[76] Stèphen C. Kleene. A symmetric form of Gödel's theorem. *Nederl. Akad. Wetensch., Proc.*, 53:800–802 = *Indagationes Math.* 12:, 244–246 (1950), 1950.

[77] Peter Koellner. Carnap on the foundations of logic and mathematics, 2009.

[78] Peter Koellner. On the question of absolute undecidability. In *Kurt Gödel: essays for his centennial*, vol. 33 of *Lect. Notes Log.*, pp. 189–225. Association of Symbolic Logic, La Jolla, CA, 2010.

[79] Henryk Kotlarski. The incompleteness theorems after 70 years. *Ann. Pure Appl. Logic*, 126(1–3):125–138, 2004.

[80] Georg Kreisel. Kurt Gödel, 1906-1978. *Biographical Memoirs of Fellows of the Royal Society*, 26:148–224, 1980. Corrigenda, 27:697, 1981; further corrigenda, 28:697, 1982.

[81] Saul Kripke. The collapse of the Hilbert Program: why a system cannot prove its own 1-consistency. *Bull. Symbolic Logic*, 15(2):229–231, 2009.

[82] Saul Kripke. The Church-Turing "thesis" as a special corollary of Gödel's completeness theorem. In B.J.Copeland, C.Posy, and O. Shagrir (eds.), *Computability—Turing, Gödel, Church, and beyond*, pp. 77–104. MIT Press, Cambridge, MA, 2013.

[83] Saul Kripke. Mathematical incompleteness results in first-order peano arithmetic: a revisionist view of the early history. *Hist. Philos. Logic*, doi:10.1080/01445340.2021.1976052. 2021.

[84] Shira Kritchman and Ran Raz. The surprise examination paradox and the second incompleteness theorem. *Notices Amer. Math. Soc.*, 57(11):1454–1458, 2010.

[85] Taishi Kurahashi. A note on derivability conditions. *J. Symb. Log.*, 85(3):1224–1253, 2020.

[86] Casimir Kuratowski. Sur l'état actuel de l'axiomatique de la théorie des ensembles. *Ann. Soc. Polon. Math.*, 3:146–147, 1925.

[87] Richard Laver. On the consistency of Borel's conjecture. *Acta Math.*, 137(3-4):151–169, 1976.

[88] Azriel Lévy. Axiom schemata of strong infinity in axiomatic set theory. *Pacific J. Math.*, 10:223–238, 1960.

[89] Martin Hugo Löb. Solution of a problem of Leon Henkin. *J. Symb. Log.*, 20:115–118, 1955.

[90] John R. Lucas. Metamathematics and the philosophy of mind: a rejoinder. *Philos. Sci.*, 38:310–313, 1971.

[91] Nikolai Luzin. Sur les ensembles projectifs de m. henri lebesgue. 180(2):1572–1574, 1925.

[92] Angus Macintyre. The impact of Gödel's incompleteness theorems on mathematics. In M. Baaz, C. H. Papadimitriou, H. W. Putnam, D. S. Scott, and C. L. Harper, Jr. (eds.), *Kurt Gödel and the foundations of mathematics*, pp. 3–25. Cambridge University Press, Cambridge, 2011.

[93] Penelope Maddy. *Defending the axioms: on the philosophical foundations of set theory*. Oxford University Press, Oxford, 2011.

[94] Anatoly I. Mal'tsev. Untersuchungen aus dem Gebiete der mathematischen Logik. *Rec. Math. Moscou, n. Ser.*, 1:323–336, 1936.

[95] Donald A. Martin. Measurable cardinals and analytic games. *Fund. Math.*, 66:287–291, 1969/1970.

[96] Donald A. Martin. Borel determinacy. *Ann. of Math. (2)*, 102(2): 363–371, 1975.

[97] Donald A. Martin and John R. Steel. Projective determinacy. *Proc. Nat. Acad. Sci. U.S.A.*, 85(18):6582–6586, 1988.

[98] Juri V. Matijasevič. The Diophantineness of enumerable sets. *Dokl. Akad. Nauk SSSR*, 191:279–282, 1970.

[99] Kenneth McAloon. Consistency results about ordinal definability. *Ann. Math. Logic*, 2(4):449–467, 1970/1971.

[100] Yiannis N. Moschovakis. *Descriptive set theory*, 2nd edn., vol. 155 of *Mathematical Surveys and Monographs*. American Mathematical Society, Providence, RI, 2009.

[101] Yiannis N. Moschovakis. Kleene's amazing second recursion theorem. *Bull. Symbolic Logic*, 16(2):189–239, 2010.

[102] Andrzej Mostowski. On recursive models of formalised arithmetic. *Bull. Acad. Polon. Sci. Cl. III*, 5:705–710, LXII, 1957.

[103] Andrzej Mostowski. *Thirty years of foundational studies: lectures on the development of mathematical logic and the study of the foundations of mathematics in 1930–1964*. Acta Philosophica Fennica, Fasc. XVII. Barnes & Noble, Inc., New York, 1966.

[104] Andrzej Mostowski. *Sentences undecidable in formalized arithmetic*. Greenwood Press, Westport, CT, 1982. An exposition of the theory of Kurt Gödel. Reprint of the 1952 original.

[105] John Myhill and Dana Scott. Ordinal definability. In *Axiomatic Set Theory (Proc. Sympos. Pure Math., Vol. XIII, Part I)*, University of California, Los Angeles, CA, 1967), pp. 271–278. American Mathematical Society, Providence, RI, 1971.

[106] Jeff Paris and Leo Harrington. A mathematical incompleteness in Peano arithmetic. In *Handbook of mathematical logic*, vol. 90 of *Stud. Logic Found. Math.*, Jon Barwise & H. Jerome Keisler (eds.) pp. 1133–1142. North-Holland, Amsterdam, 1977.

[107] Charles Parsons. Platonism and mathematical intuition in Kurt Gödel's thought. *Bull. Symb. Log.*, 1(1):44–74, 1995.

[108] Orlando Patterson. *Slavery and Social Death: A Comparative Study*. Harvard University Press, Cambridge, MA, 2018.

[109] Roger Penrose. *Shadows of the mind: a search for the missing science of consciousness*. Oxford University Press, Oxford, 1994.

[110] Panu Raatikainen. Hilbert's Program revisited. *Synthese*, 137 (special issue): 157–177, 2000.

[111] Abraham Robinson. On languages which are based on non-standard arithmetic. *Nagoya Math. J.*, 22:83–117, 1963.

[112] Julia Robinson. Existential definability in arithmetic. *Trans. Amer. Math. Soc.*, 72:437–449, 1952.

[113] Barkley Rosser. Extensions of some theorems of Gödel and Church. *J. Symb. Log.*, 1(3):87–91, 1936.

[114] Saeed Salehi. On the diagonal lemma of Gödel and Carnap. *Bull. Symb. Log.*, 26(1):80–88, 2020.

[115] Saharon Shelah. Every two elementarily equivalent models have isomorphic ultrapowers. *Israel J. Math.*, 10:224–233, 1971.

[116] Saharon Shelah. Infinite abelian groups, Whitehead problem and some constructions. *Israel J. Math.*, 18:243–256, 1974.

[117] Wilfried Sieg. Gödel on computability. *Philos. Math.*, 14:189–207, 2006.

[118] Waclaw Sierpinski. Sur un ensemble non denombrable, dont toute image continue est de mesure nulle. *Fund. Math.*, 11:302–304, 1928.

[119] Stephen G. Simpson. Nonprovability of certain combinatorial properties of finite trees. In L. Harrington, M. Morley, A. Sĉêdrov, and S. Simpson (eds.), *Harvey Friedman's research on the foundations of mathematics*, vol. 117 of *Studies in Logic and the Foundations of Mathematics*, pp. 87–117. North-Holland, Amsterdam, 1985.

[120] Craig Smoryński. Lectures on nonstandard models of arithmetic. In G. Lolli, G. Longo, and A. Marcja (eds.), *Logic colloquium '82*

(Florence, 1982), volume 112 of *Studies in Logic and Foundations of Mathematics*, pp. 1–70. North-Holland, Amsterdam, 1984.

[121] Raymond M. Smullyan. *Theory of formal systems*. Annals of Mathematics Studies, No. 47. Princeton University Press, Princeton, NJ, 1961.

[122] William W. Tait. Gödel on intuition and on Hilbert's finitism. In S. Feferman, C. Parsons, and S. G. Simpson (eds.), *Kurt Gödel: essays for his centennial*, vol. 33 of *Lecture Notes in Logic*, pp. 88–108. Association of Symbolic Logic La Jolla, CA, 2010.

[123] Alfred Tarski. Sur les ensembles définissables de nombres réels. *Fund. Math.*, (7):210–239, 1931.

[124] Alfred Tarski. Der Wahrheitsbegriff in den formalisierten Sprachen. *Studia Philosophica*, 1:261–405, 1936.

[125] Alfred Tarski. *Undecidable theories*. Studies in Logic and the Foundations of Mathematics. North-Holland Publishing Co., Amsterdam, 1968. In collaboration with Andrzej Mostowski and Raphael M. Robinson, second printing.

[126] Richard Tieszen. Gödel and the intuition of concepts. *Synthese*, 133(3):363–391, 2002.

[127] Alan M. Turing. On computable numbers, with an application to the Entscheidungsproblem. *Proc. London Math. Soc.*, S2-42(1):230.

[128] Alan M. Turing. Systems of logic based on ordinals. *Proc. London Math. Soc. (2)*, 45(3):161–228, 1939.

[129] Mark van Atten. *Essays on Gödel's reception of Leibniz, Husserl, and Brouwer*, vol. 35 of Logic, Epistemology, and the Unity of Science. Springer, Cham, 2015.

[130] Mark van Atten and Juliette Kennedy. On the philosophical development of Kurt Gödel. *Bull. Symb. Log.*, 9(4):425–476, 2003.

[131] Mark van Atten and Juliette Kennedy. "Gödel's modernism: on set-theoretic incompleteness," revisited. In S. Lindström, E. Palmgren, K. Segerberg, and V. Stoltenberg-Hansen (eds.), *Logicism, intuitionism, and formalism*, vol. 341 of *Synthese Library*, pp. 303–355. Springer, Dordrecht, 2009.

[132] Robert L. Vaught. Alfred Tarski's work in model theory. *J. Symb. Log.*, 51(4):869–882, 1986.

[133] Robert L. Vaught. Errata: "Alfred Tarski's work in model theory." *J. Symb. Log.* 52(4):vii, 1987.

[134] Giorgio Venturi and Matteo Viale. New axioms in set theory. *Mat. Cult. Soc. Riv. Unione Mat. Ital. (I)*, 3(3):211–236, 2018.

[135] Albert Visser. From Tarski to Gödel – or how to derive the second incompleteness theorem from the undefinability of truth without self-reference. *J. Logic Comput.*, 29(5):595–604, 2019.

[136] Hao Wang. *A logical journey: representation and mind.* MIT Press, Cambridge, MA, 1996.

[137] Andreas Weiermann. Phase transitions for Gödel incompleteness. *Ann. Pure Appl. Logic*, 157(2-3):281–296, 2009.

[138] Jan Woleński. Gödel, Tarski and the undefinability of truth. *Jbuch. Kurt-Gödel-Ges.*, pp. 97–108 (1993), 1991.

[139] Hugh Woodin. In search of Ultimate-L: the 19th Midrasha Mathematicae Lectures. *Bull. Symb. Log.*, 23(1):1–109, 2017.

[140] W. Hugh Woodin. Supercompact cardinals, sets of reals, and weakly homogeneous trees. *Proc. Nat. Acad. Sci. U.S.A.*, 85(18):6587–6591, 1988.

[141] Richard Zach. Hilbert's Program. In E. N. Zalta (ed.), *The Stanford Encyclopedia of Philosophy*. Metaphysics Research Lab, Stanford University, Stanford, CA, 2003.

[142] Ernst Zermelo. Über Grenzzahlen und Mengenbereiche. Neue Untersuchungen über die Grundlagen der Mengenlehre. *Fundam. Math.*, 16:29–47, 1930.

Acknowledgements

I would like to thank my husband, the logician Jouko Väänänen, who joined me on much of the research for this Element; Balthasar Grabmayr, who read a late draft of this Element very carefully, making many helpful suggestions and improvements; and finally I would like to thank an anonymous referee who also made helpful suggestions for improvement. I am grateful to Juliet Floyd and Zeynep Soysal for helpful correspondence, also about Carnap's notion of syntax, and to Patricia Blanchette and Penelope Maddy for helpful discussions about strong representability.

This Element is dedicated to my niece Miranda Delahoy, epidemiologist and humanitarian on the front lines of the COVID pandemic.

Cambridge Elements ☰

Philosophy and Logic

Bradley Armour-Garb

SUNY Albany

Brad Armour-Garb is chair and Professor of Philosophy at SUNY Albany. His books
include *The Law of Non-Contradiction* (co-edited with Graham Priest and J. C. Beall,
2004), *Deflationary Truth and Deflationism and Paradox* (both co-edited with J. C. Beall,
2005), *Pretense and Pathology* (with James Woodbridge, Cambridge University Press,
2015), *Reflections on the Liar* (2017), and *Fictionalism in Philosophy* (co-edited with
Frederick Kroon, 2020).

Frederick Kroon

The University of Auckland

Frederick Kroon is Emeritus Professor of Philosophy at the University of Auckland. He has
authored numerous papers in formal and philosophical logic, ethics, philosophy of
language, and metaphysics, and is the author of *A Critical Introduction to Fictionalism*
(with Stuart Brock and Jonathan McKeown-Green, 2018).

About the Series

This Cambridge Elements series provides an extensive overview of the many and varied
connections between philosophy and logic. Distinguished authors provide an up-to-date
summary of the results of current research in their fields and give their own take on what
they believe are the most significant debates influencing research, drawing original
conclusions.

Cambridge Elements $\equiv$

Philosophy and Logic

Printed in the United States
by Baker & Taylor Publisher Services